COMPREHENSIVE RESEARCH
AND STUDY GUIDE

Percy Bysshe Shelley

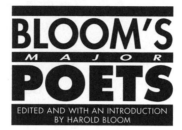

BLOOM'S

MAJOR

POETS

EDITED AND WITH AN INTRODUCTION
BY HAROLD BLOOM

CURRENTLY AVAILABLE

BLOOM'S MAJOR SHORT STORY WRITERS

Anton Chekhov
Joseph Conrad
Stephen Crane
William Faulkner
F. Scott Fitzgerald
Nathaniel Hawthorne
Ernest Hemingway
O. Henry
Shirley Jackson
Henry James
James Joyce
D. H. Lawrence
Jack London
Herman Melville
Flannery O'Connor
Edgar Allan Poe
Katherine Anne Porter
J. D. Salinger
John Steinbeck
Mark Twain
John Updike
Eudora Welty

BLOOM'S MAJOR WORLD POETS

Maya Angelou
Robert Browning
Geoffrey Chaucer
Samuel T. Coleridge
Dante
Emily Dickinson
John Donne
T. S. Eliot
Robert Frost
Homer
Langston Hughes
John Keats
John Milton
Sylvia Plath
Edgar Allan Poe
Poets of World War I
Shakespeare's Poems & Sonnets
Percy Shelley
Alfred, Lord Tennyson
Walt Whitman
William Wordsworth
William Butler Yeats

COMPREHENSIVE RESEARCH
AND STUDY GUIDE

Percy Bysshe Shelley

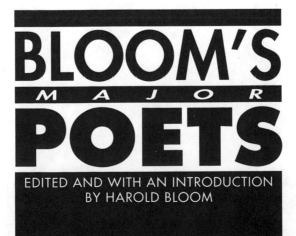

BLOOM'S
MAJOR
POETS

EDITED AND WITH AN INTRODUCTION
BY HAROLD BLOOM

© 2001 by Chelsea House Publishers, a subsidiary of
Haights Cross Communications.

Introduction © 2001 by Harold Bloom.

Printed and bound in the United States of America.

First Printing
1 3 5 7 9 8 6 4 2

Library of Congress Cataloging-in-Publication Data
applied for:

ISBN 0-7910-5930-8

Chelsea House Publishers
1974 Sproul Road, Suite 400
Broomall, PA 19008-0914

The Chelsea House World Wide Web address is
http://www.chelseahouse.com

Contributing Editor: Janyce Marson

Produced by: Robert Gerson Publisher's Services, Santa Barbara, CA

Contents

User's Guide

This volume is designed to present biographical, critical, and bibliographical information on the author's best-known or most important poems. Following Harold Bloom's editor's note and introduction is a detailed biography of the author, discussing major life events and important literary accomplishments. A thematic and structural analysis of each poem follows, tracing significant themes, patterns, and motifs in the work.

A selection of critical extracts, derived from previously published material from leading critics, analyzes aspects of each poem. The extracts consist of statements from the author, if available, early reviews of the work, and later evaluations up to the present. A bibliography of the author's writings (including a complete list of all books written, cowritten, edited, and translated), a list of additional books and articles on the author and the work, and an index of themes and ideas in the author's writings conclude the volume.

~

Harold Bloom is Sterling Professor of the Humanities at Yale University and Henry W. and Albert A. Berg Professor of English at the New York University Graduate School. He is the author of over 20 books, including *Shelley's Mythmaking* (1959), *The Visionary Company* (1961), *Blake's Apocalypse* (1963), *Yeats* (1970), *A Map of Misreading* (1975), *Kabbalah and Criticism* (1975), *Agon: Toward a Theory of Revisionism* (1982), *The American Religion* (1992), *The Western Canon* (1994), and *Omens of Millennium: The Gnosis of Angels, Dreams, and Resurrection* (1996). *The Anxiety of Influence* (1973) sets forth Professor Bloom's provocative theory of the literary relationships between the great writers and their predecessors. His most recent books include *Shakespeare: The Invention of the Human,* a 1998 National Book Award finalist, and *How to Read and Why,* which was published in 2000.

Professor Bloom earned his Ph.D. from Yale University in 1955 and has served on the Yale faculty since then. He is a 1985 MacArthur Foundation Award recipient, served as the Charles Eliot Norton Professor of Poetry at Harvard University in 1987–88, and has received honorary degrees from the universities of Rome and Bologna. In 1999, Professor Bloom received the prestigious American Academy of Arts and Letters Gold Medal for Criticism.

Currently, Harold Bloom is the editor of numerous Chelsea House volumes of literary criticism, including the series BLOOM'S NOTES, BLOOM'S MAJOR DRAMATISTS, BLOOM'S MAJOR NOVELISTS, MAJOR LITERARY CHARACTERS, MODERN CRITICAL VIEWS, MODERN CRITICAL INTERPRETATIONS, and WOMEN WRITERS OF ENGLISH AND THEIR WORKS.

Editor's Note

My Introduction speculates upon Shelley's very individual Gnosticism, his heretical version of a non-Christian transcendence. Shelley's "Ode to the West Wind" and *The Triumph of Life* are interpreted in the context of his lifelong struggle with Wordsworth's influence.

As there are twenty-nine critical views on five major poems, I remark here only upon some that I find particularly interesting and useful.

Anne Janowitz considers "Ozymandias" against the background of nineteenth-century Egyptology, while Diana Hendry meditates upon the problematic nature of Shelley's skylark.

Jennifer Wagner emphasizes the reader's centrality in "Ode to the West Wind" after which G. K. Blank sees the poem as a Shelleyan triumph over the anxiety of influence.

On "Adonais" I particularly commend Peter Sacks and Neil Arditi, who balance the poem's originality against its sources, both literary and experiential.

David Quint illuminates "The Triumph of Life" in his investigation of pageantry in the poem.

Introduction

HAROLD BLOOM

Shelley was a lyric and Pindaric poet who desired to write revolutionary epic and lyrical drama. At heart a skeptic and not a Platonic visionary, he nevertheless broke through to a Gnostic vision very much his own, curiously parallel to the work of William Blake, whom he never read.

A. D. Nuttall, in his *Alternative Trinities*, studies Christopher Marlowe, John Milton, and Blake as three intricate instances of poetic heresies that approach Gnosticism. The Gnostic religion, to most scholars, is a Second Century of the Common Era Christian heresy. I myself agree with Henry Corbin, who argued that Gnosticism (or esotericism) was an eclectic world religion, and the truest form therefore of Islam, Christianity, and Judaism.

Perhaps Shelley's *gnosis*, his poetic way of knowing, was not altogether a Gnosticism, but his visionary drama *Prometheus Unbound* opposes Jupiter as a kind of Gnostic *archon* or Demiurge to Prometheus as a Gnostic savior, almost indeed a Stranger or Alien God.

Shelley's magnificent "Ode to the West Wind," composed between the Third and Fourth Acts of *Prometheus Unbound*, demands to be read on several levels of interpretation: political, personal, heretical-religious, and agonistic in relation to Shelley's poetic precursors, John Milton and William Wordsworth in particular. Politically, Shelley was of the permanent Left: almost the Leon Trotsky of his day. Yet Shelley's personal stance strangely blended hope and despair. Like Job, the poet falls upon the thorns of life, and he prays to the wind to lift him as a leaf, a wave, a cloud, as anything but a human being. From this nadir, Shelley makes a great recovery when he urges the West Wind to make him its lyre, and to be "through my lips . . . the trumpet of a prophecy." A revolutionary spirit, the West Wind is also the harbinger of a Gnostic revelation, correcting the Creation-Fall by going beyond nature.

I suspect that Shelley's deepest struggle in the poem is with Wordsworth, the prophet of nature, whose "sober coloring" is answered by the "Ode to the West Wind"'s "deep autumnal tone."

Shelley's impatient and apocalyptic temperament will not wait upon Nature's revelation of herself.

Shelley set himself against Milton in *Prometheus Unbound* and against Wordsworth in the "Hymn to Intellectual Beauty," "Mont Blanc," and the "Ode to the West Wind." In his final poem, the great death-march of the fragmentary *The Triumph of Life*, Shelley turned to Dante, whose *Inferno* and *Purgatorio* provided the context for a vision of judgment. Shelley hymns the triumph of life over individual human integrity, while showing how the natural sun blots out the light of the stars, or poetic imagination, while the sun itself vanishes in the glare of the cold Chariot of Life. Something like a new Gnostic heresy is darkly suggested by Shelley's last vision, a Sublime fragment but profoundly despairing of any hope in ordinary human life. ❀

Biography of
Percy Bysshe Shelley

The year 1813 was momentous for young Percy Bysshe Shelley. Besides becoming a disciple of the radical social philosopher William Godwin, Shelley's first poetic work, *Queen Mab*, was printed privately. This work is a long romantic poem that describes the journey of the disembodied soul of a young girl named Ianthe. As she travels through space, the guiding spirit Mab reveals to her a series of visions. These visions are of a bleak past in which humanity is seen as transitory and irrelevant; an awful present dominated by tyrannical kings, political sycophants, and the social evils of institutionalized religion; and a utopian future in which humanity's potential for perfection will be realized through a liberal education and a progressive science that will improve the physical environment.

In 1813 Shelley also fell in love with Godwin's daughter, the beautiful Mary Wollstonecraft (who would one day write the popular Gothic novel *Frankenstein*). At the time, Shelley was still married to Harriet Westbrook, a woman with whom he had eloped with in 1811 when she was only sixteen years old. He had married Harriet to save her from a "tyrannical" father, and he had vowed to love her forever, but now he fled to France with Mary Wollstonecraft and her stepsister, Claire Clairmont.

Like his friend William Godwin, Shelley was opposed to the institution of marriage as yet another form of tyranny and codified degradation, but despite this philosophy, he entered his second marriage to Mary Wollstonecraft in 1818. Still believing in non-exclusive love, Shelley invited Harriet to live with them as a "sister." Harriet, however, pregnant by another lover, sank into a depression and drowned herself. As for Shelley, he became a social outcast with a reputation for being both an atheist and an immoralist. He had children with both his wives, but he was denied custody of the two children from his marriage with Harriet. Feeling rejected by society, Shelley moved to Italy and continued his restless existence there, wandering from place to place.

Percy Bysshe Shelley, the radical nonconformist, was born in 1792 to a conservative aristocratic family. His grandfather, Sir Bysshe Shelley, had made himself the richest man in Horsham, Sussex, and his father, Timothy Shelley, was a conventional Member of Parliament. In fact, Percy Shelley was in line for a baronetcy.

Percy's education began at age six under the direction of his tutor, Reverend Edwards, a Welsh parson. Percy received a traditional Welsh instruction from Reverend Edwards; as a part of that, he also learned Latin and Greek. In 1802, his family sent him to Sion House Academy, Brentford, a rather odd choice for an aristocratic education, since many of the boys were tradesmen's sons. From there, he went to Eton in 1804.

At Eton, Shelley received a classical education, becoming particularly adept in Latin verse. While at Eton, he began reading Gothic mysteries, tales of horror that included such elements as vampirism, violence, eroticism, magical spells, and strange and gloomy settings—for instance, haunted castles and treacherous journeys. Shelley also developed a keen interest in science, including such things as electrical machines and fire-balloons.

He was especially attracted to the scientific lectures given at Eton by Adam Walker, a self-taught man who enchanted the schoolboys' imaginations with the "marvels" of science. Walker was not afraid to make bold speculations when the facts did not prove him right.

But the most influential thinker for Shelley at this time was Dr. James Lind, a scientist and traveler who visited China as a naval surgeon in the 1760s; in 1772 he also accompanied Sir Joseph Banks on a scientific expedition to Iceland. Lind, a tall, white-haired man over seventy years of age, was friends with some of the most important scientists of his day (such as James Watt, who worked with the steam engine). Lind was an eccentric man who encouraged rebellious attitudes. He even owned his own printing press and was suspected of publishing subversive pamphlets. But above all else, Lind was a free-spirited and benevolent mentor for the young Shelley, who engaged in long conversations with Lind on the writings of the English political theorist William Godwin and the doctor/poet Erasmus Darwin.

Despite these stimulating relationships, Shelley's time at Eton was not entirely happy. Slight of build and unskilled in sports, Shelley was often the target of older and stronger boys. For the sensitive young Shelley, the bullies and abusive schoolmasters of his early schooldays served as early representatives of people's general inhumanity to each other. Shelley recorded recollections of these schoolboy days in the dedication to *Laon and Cythna* (later called *The Revolt of Islam*): "So without shame, I spake:— 'I will be wise, / And just, and free, and mild' . . . I then controlled / My tears, my heart grew calm, and I was meek and bold."

While he was at Eton, Shelley published his first story, *Zastrozz*, a romance. He left Eton just before his eighteenth birthday, and entered Oxford University where he continued to be a voracious reader and writer. His second romance, *St. Irvyne*, was published in April 1810. He also worked with his sister Elizabeth to write the poem "Victor and Cazire."

At Oxford in the autumn of 1810, Shelley's closest friend was Thomas Jefferson Hogg, a self-confident young man who shared Shelley's love of philosophy and rejection of orthodoxy. The two friends centered their serious reading on Plato, Locke, and Hume. The latter two philosophers bolstered their confidence that their religious skepticism was justified. In fact, the two friends collaborated on a pamphlet, *The Necessity of Atheism*, which claimed that God's existence could not be proven on empirical grounds (by mere observation or experience) and further, that "no degree of criminality is attachable to disbelief." Needless to say, this pamphlet created shock waves and the university demanded a retraction of the ideas it promulgated. However, while James Hogg capitulated to pressure from both Oxford and his family to repudiate this pamphlet, Shelley refused. In fact, Shelley went so far as to send the pamphlet to all the bishops and other significant faculty members and administrators at Oxford, many of whom were devout churchmen. He was hoping to receive counterarguments from them, but it was a naïve act.

As a result of his rebellion, Shelley was expelled from Oxford in 1811. His career at Oxford lasted a mere six months and the events surrounding his expulsion caused an ever-widening rift with his father. In the end, Thomas Hogg admitted that he was equally involved with the pamphlet scheme, and he was also expelled. The two young men left for London on March 26, 1811, and took lodgings in Poland Street.

Once he arrived in London, Shelley was faced with the difficult task of reconciling with his father. The Shelley baronetcy was only five years old, and Percy's father wanted no further blots on the family reputation. He demanded that his son return home to be placed under very strict supervision. This left Shelley with a brief dilemma as he could not desert his beloved friend, Thomas Hogg, simply because his father ordered him to do so.

However, that dilemma ended in April when Hogg left London to pursue a legal education at York. Alone now in London, Percy was overwhelmed with homesickness, and this loneliness caused him to set out for home. Midway, however, he broke off his journey and instead stayed with his uncle, Captain Pilford, a veteran of the battle at Trafalgar. His father's communications with him were still very frosty, so Shelley went next to visit his cousin, Thomas Groves, in Wales. That visit also ended abruptly, and now Percy's attentions turned to Harriet Westbrook, whom he had met some six months earlier during his stay in London.

Theirs was a hasty and foolish marriage fueled by his father's rebuke and his own renegade and impulsive personality. The breach with his father now became even deeper. While Shelley was willing to be reconciled with his father, he would not make hypocritical statements for the sake of restoring their relationship. Fortunately, Captain Pilfold was fond of his nephew, and he provided the means for the young couple's subsistence in Edinburgh.

Shortly thereafter, Hogg visited his newly wed friend at Edinburgh, and the couple, in need of money, returned to York with Hogg. Shelley regretted this later when he discovered that Hogg attempted to seduce Harriet. With Harriet's sister Eliza, the couple left York and settled in the beautiful countryside of Keswick.

This location brought Shelley close to the other Lake Poets, especially Robert Southey, with whom he had long talks. Keswick also had the added advantage of being near Greystoke Castle, the seat of the politically radical Duke of Norfolk, who had been kind to Shelley and was in a position to help Shelley become reconciled with his father. This reconciliation was accomplished in the form of a conciliatory letter to his father, and eventually, Shelley's allowance was restored.

In the following spring of June 1814, however, Shelley began to drift away from Harriet. Harriet had lost her earlier intellectual interests, and now Shelley fell desperately and insanely in love with Mary Wollstonecraft, who was also an author. This was the time of triumphal parades in London celebrating the Allied victory over

Napoleon, with English tourists flocking to Paris, a city that had previously been off limits. And so, on July 28, 1814, the two lovers followed the tide and eloped to France (along with Mary's sister, Claire Clairmont). In so doing, they enraged both Mary's father and Shelley's former mentor, William Godwin, who had now become a respectable citizen.

When they returned to London in September, they were without funds. Even worse, they had incurred serious debts from unscrupulous lenders who charged unconscionable interest. Always on the run from bailiffs and creditors, the young couple drifted from place to place. Shelley also soon realized that both the general public and his friends and family regarded him as an immoral atheist. On top of all these stresses, Shelley was not in good health. Nevertheless, his insatiable reading continued despite the emotional upheavals of 1814–15.

The couple moved to Bishopsgate. In September 1815 they went on a rowing trip up the Thames from Windsor, and during this outing, the romantic scene of Lechlade churchyard resurrected Shelley's poetic inspiration. In the poem "A Summer Evening Churchyard," Shelley describes the view where "[t]he wind has swept from the wide atmosphere / Each vapour that obscured the sunset's ray; / And pallid Evening twines its beaming hair." His second long poem, "Alastor; or, The Spirit of Solitude," was likewise written at Virginia Water in the autumn of 1815. "Alastor" is a poem that deals with a young, solitary, and innocent man who finds joy and tranquility in nature until he becomes aware of his isolation and realizes his need to communicate with others. In this poem Shelley's particular fondness for water imagery becomes prominent. Unfortunately, "Alastor" did not receive favorable reviews when in was published in 1816. Looking for diversion, Shelley decided on a holiday abroad, with Italy as the first destination.

On this trip, when he reached Geneva, Shelley first met Byron in May 1816. Byron was 28 at the time and Shelley was now 23; both bore the unpleasant memory of failed marriages and a grievance against aristocratic pretense. However, the good fortune of his meeting with Byron was overshadowed by terrible tragedy in 1816—the death of Fanny Godwin from an overdose of laudanum, followed by the suicide of his first wife Harriet. Her body was found in the Serpentine in London.

Her death, however, left Shelley free to marry Mary in 1818. Shortly thereafter, they moved to Italy, and from that time forward Shelley saw himself as a social outcast from the human race. He resumed his restless wandering, moving from house to house. Within nine months' time, tragedy struck again; he and Mary had two children, Clara and William, and now they both died. Mary was left utterly distraught and even the birth of another child, Percy Florence, could not entirely heal her tremendous pain.

Following these tragedies, however, Shelley wrote some of his greatest poetry and prose, including his masterpiece, *Prometheus Unbound,* a play that dramatizes the suffering of Prometheus, the ancient Greek god who was punished for stealing fire from heaven in order to give it to mankind. He also wrote "Adonais," a brilliant elegy on the death of his beloved poet, John Keats, and a very important critical work, *A Defence of Poetry.*

When the Shelleys settled in Pisa in 1820, the poet had finally achieved a contentment he had not known during his adult life. Gathered round him were his "Pisana Circle" of friends, which included Lord Byron and the handsome young Edward Trelawny. But the end of his life came abruptly, in a way reminiscent of "Adonais," when the boat in which Shelley and his friend Edward Williams were sailing overturned during a violent squall on July 8, 1822. Their bodies were found several days later, and Shelley's ashes were buried in the Protestant Cemetery in Rome. His death, ironically, left unfinished what promised to be his greatest achievement, "The Triumph of Life." ❀

Thematic Analysis of
"Ozymandias"

Written sometime in late 1817 and published on January 11, 1818 in Leigh Hunt's *Examiner*, "Ozymandias" is a poem that bears the Greek name for the Egyptian Pharaoh, Ramses II (13th century B.C.). In addition to his wars with the Hittites and Libyans, Ramses is known for his extensive building projects, as well as the many colossal statues of him throughout Egypt. His reign marked the height of Egypt's imperial power. According to Diodorus Siculus, a Greek historian of the 1st century B.C., the largest statue in Egypt bore the inscription, "I am Ozymandias, king of kings; if anyone wishes to know what I am and where I lie, let him surpass me in some of my exploits." A controversy continues today regarding the 19th-century's unquestioning reliance on the identity of Diodorus's sources; few of his sources survive outside his own work, making it difficult to ascertain who or what is being quoted verbatim.

The 19th century developed a great interest in the ancient Egyptian culture, and that interest was the beginning of modern Egyptology. In the 1820s, Jean-François Champollion deciphered the Egyptian hieroglyphic writing on the newly discovered Rosetta Stone. Prior to Champollion's discovery, the historical events of the early 19th century helped to awaken an interest in this ancient culture. When Napoleon invaded Egypt in 1798, he was accompanied by a group of 150 scientists and artists who came along to survey the newly conquered territory. Furthermore, in 1806 Mohammed Ali, a soldier of fortune, installed himself as pasha (a man of great rank) of Egypt, and during his long reign, he encouraged artistic competition between the French and English, resulting in a flood of Egypt artifacts in both Europe and America.

Shelley's own interest in Egyptology is manifested in many of his poems, such as *Alastor; or, the Spirit of Solitude*, where the young poet, who has gone in search of the origin of things, journeys to Egypt and Abyssinia, to the origin of writing. "His wander step, / Obedient to high thoughts, has visited / The awful ruins of the days of old: . . . Of Babylon, the eternal pyramids, Memphis and Thebes, and whatsoe'er of strange / Sculptured on alabaster obelisk, . . . or mutilated sphinx."

Ancient Egyptian culture was a civilization obsessed with death and personal survival, an obsession indicated by its foremost occupation—the construction of inscribed funerary monuments—pyramids, tombs, obelisks, stelae, and sarcophagi. It was a culture obsessed with time, and its fascination with the afterlife influenced all its earthly work and effort. These themes are prominent in "Ozymandias." It is simultaneously a poem concerned with poetic effort and the anxiety of whether that effort will be remembered.

The most significant key to understanding Shelley's agenda in "Ozymandias" resides in the verb "to mock." *To mock* most frequently means to treat an object, person, or idea with contempt or ridicule. It also means to imitate that object, usually for derision, or to produce an insincere or counterfeit version of the original object. Interestingly, a rather obscure meaning of the word "mock," the origin of which is unknown, identifies the word with a stump and root of a tree, or refers to a large stick of wood, especially that burned at Christmas. Thus, Shelley's play on the word "mock" makes this poem, in one sense, a pun—a rhetorical device that depends on similarity of sound for a multiplicity of meaning. This device, like the subject matter of the poem, was familiar to the classical world and much discussed and written about in its rhetorical treatises. As will be seen, "Ozymandias" utilizes puns to explore a variety of issues concerning the ravages of time and the effacement of memory.

Beginning with the first line, the narrating voice creates doubt as to the chronological time in which his poem is set, stating that "I met a traveller from an antique land." The word antique creates the first ambiguity in the poem. Is the traveler a tourist living in the 19th century who merely refers to Egypt as the ancient world or is there some time warp in which the narrator meets with an actual inhabitant of antiquity? At the very least, we are left a bit disconcerted as to the temporal location of this poem.

In the next two lines, we see Shelley's adept and very oblique application of a "mock" as a stump of a tree, when the strange visitor reports that "Two vast and trunkless legs of stone / Stand in the desert." At the same time, Shelley also introduces us to the multi-faceted symbols and images he will employ to convey the erosive effects of time. First, time has "amputated" this monument so that its representational value, a sculpture of a former ruler of this very same country, is seriously curtailed. Second, this sculpture is to be found in the desert, an arid and lifeless terrain, and as it is made of stone, it is also very much of the desert as well, its stony composition reminding us that its physicality is inextricably linked to the same disintegrative processes that cause rocks to turn into silt. And finally, we are given additional details of this "amputation," in a series of disturbing images: "Near them, on the sand, / Half sunk a shattered visage lies, whose frown, / And wrinkled lip, and sneer of cold command." Indeed, time has now grown violent, determined to annihilate any physical evidence that this person ever lived.

Most interesting is Shelley's use of the word "visage" in reference to Ozymandias's face, a word derived from the Latin *visus*, meaning sight or appearance, and in English defined not only as the front part of the face, but an aspect of the person's true character and emotions. Through the multiple meanings of this word, Shelley introduces the theme of a former leader whose monument has fallen into ruin and disgrace, one who was arrogant, mean-spirited, and tyrannical. These images of Ramses II are all appropriate. He was a king of nonroyal origin, appointed at a very young age by his father Seti I; his reign was the last peak of Egyptian imperialism, an important fact for the radical Shelley, who opposed all forms of political tyranny and aggrandizement, most notably Napoleon's political agenda.

Finally, Shelley uses one further meaning of the word *visage*, referring to something done merely for outward show, a falsehood of sorts. This indicates two important points: First, as the traveler tells us, the ancient sculptor did a brilliant job reading Ramses II ("its sculptor well those passions read / Which yet survive, stamped on these lifeless things, / The hand that mocked them, and the heart that fed"). Thus, art remains the repository of truth; despite Ramses' obsessions with public works to celebrate his achievements, the artist captured his real character. Second, though the statue is in a state of ruin, the truth nevertheless remains with a tenacity that is as irrepressible as the one it represents, and this truth will indeed withstand all attempts to obliterate it. ("And on the pedestal, these words appear: / My name is Ozymandias, King of Kings, / Look on my Works, ye Mighty, and despair! Nothing beside remains.")

And so Ozymandias's decaying statue, exposed to the elements and to human scrutiny, is left "boundless and bare / The lone and level sands stretch[ing] far away." This very same sand, commonly used to measure time, has curiously lost that ability in a poem that is ultimately timeless. Indeed, for a powerful political leader, such as Ramses II and Napoleon, what is recorded and memorialized in the chronicles of history are the deeds they performed and the character traits that motivated those actions. ❀

Critical Views on
"Ozymandias"

ANNE JANOWITZ ON THE 19TH-CENTURY INTEREST
IN EGYPTOLOGY

[Anne Janowitz is the editor of *Romanticism and Gender* (1998) and *Lyric and Labour in the Romantic Tradition* (1998). In the excerpt below from her article, "Shelley's Monument to 'Ozymandias,'" Janowitz discusses the poem within the context of the 19th-century interest in Egyptology and the way in which it "took firm hold of the English imagination."]

Though "Egyptianisms" figure importantly in English taste from the mid-eighteenth century, it was in the aftermath of the Napoleonic expedition, with the publication of the French Commission's *Description de L'Egypte* and the 1803 translation into English of Dominique Vivant Denon's *Voyage dans la Basse et la Haute Egypte* that the Egyptian revival—a delight in any and all "Egyptianisms"— took firm hold of the English imagination. With the arrival of a myriad of Egyptian artefacts and ruined monuments at the British Museum, it is not surprising that Shelley and his friend Horace Smith would participate in the fashion by composing poems on the theme of Egyptian ruins. Shelley's sonnet to Ozymandias has fared better than Smith's, and is now a classroom staple—a distilled example of Shelley's anti-tyrannical political position.

Shelley deftly evokes both the pride and the fall of this Egyptian ruler by citing the Pharaoh's commissioned inscription—intended to discourage any who would try to conquer him—in a landscape of sand, the dust to which both Ozymandias' "works" and nature itself have been reduced through the workings of time. The only survivor of this devastation is the skill of the tyrant's sculptor, whose rendering of Ozymandias' passions—witnessed in his "frown" and "sneer of cold command"—survives through time and endures as the defeated Pharaoh's monument.

What critical attention has been paid to the poem consists primarily in scholars' attempts to decide upon its exact source, and the various investigations of D. W. Thompson, Johnstone Parr, and others concur that while Diodorus of Sicily's *Library of History* must be granted to be the originary source, the large number of eighteenth-century and early nineteenth-century travel accounts of Egypt may also be considered appropriate mediate sources for Shelley's sonnet. Yet, as H. M. Richmond points out, what had been merely a "series of random observations" in travelers' accounts "became in Shelley's mind a brilliantly symbolic unity, fused by his passionate hatred of tyrants and his desire to pass judgment on their aspirations." ⟨. . .⟩

For "Ozymandias," while grounded in the familiar eighteenth-century genre of ruin poems, departs from the convention by inviting the *reader* to intuit the poem's judgment on the vanity of worldly glory as well as its judgment on the vitality of art in the face of the ravages of time, rather than making that judgment articulate. Shelley also departs from the convention of the "ruin piece" by situating his implicit moral within the thematic and formal convention of the sonnet—a form traditionally linked to the theme of the perseverance of art over time. This curious positioning provides an excellent example of what Anne Mellor has cogently defined as Romantic irony—the simultaneous decreative and recreative action which attests to the vitality of the imagination to see the world as passing both into and out of form. The rhetorical irony of Shelley's sonnet is made by juxtaposing the heroic inscription of a living tyrant with that same inscription as it becomes a dismal epitaph on the ruler's works, now reduced to dust. But within the sonnet, this passing away of the worldly is counter-balanced by the skill of the Egyptian sculptor who is able to make passions permanent and imaginatively realizable. The larger ironic gesture of the poem is to make a monument to the ephemerality of monumentality, and to keep the poem imaginatively alive by calling on the reader to articulate for him or herself Shelley's judgment on both Ozymandias and his sculptor's art. ⟨. . .⟩

As the Napoleonic expedition opened up traffic in statuary and other relics from the banks of the Nile, popular interest in the mysteries of Egypt burgeoned; and in that efflorescence, a great number of travel journals and site descriptions flooded the English reading public. Shelley's poem evoking the scattered remains of Ozymandias occupies a unique place among the tributes to Egyptian remnants, for in an ironic footnote to the history of the poem in

England, Shelley's sonnet on the ruined colossus was subsequently invoked by later writers as proof of the statue's existence, while its actual site and physical presence was, at best, vague. ⟨. . .⟩

One striking feature that emerges from the investigations into Shelley's source for the poem, and from a survey of the eighteenth and early nineteenth-century accounts of travelers to Egypt, is how closely and ambiguously intertwined were first-hand descriptions of sites along the Nile with earlier, classical descriptions of the same sites. In the exchange between travelers' journals and the classical texts which provided the historical map to Egypt, the actual monument of Ozymandias recedes further and further into physical obscurity. If we follow the path of references to Ozymandias from its classical source in Diodorus of Sicily's *Library of History* to its place in Shelley's sonnet, we will see more clearly the place of "Ozymandias" as a particularly Romantic example of the Egyptian Revival.

> —Anne Janowitz, "Shelley's Monument to Ozymandias," *Philological Quarterly* 63, no. 4 (Fall 1984): pp. 477–479.

Albert C. Labriola on the Art of Sculpture in the Poem

[Albert C. Labriola is the author of *Milton's Legacy in the Arts* (1988). In the excerpt below from his article, "Sculptural Poetry: The Visual Imagination of Michelangelo, Keats, and Shelley," Labriola discusses "Ozymandias" as a poem which is concerned with sculpture and the art of sculpturing, a theme which necessarily becomes a discussion of the art of interpretation.]

Though studies of visual imagery in literature abound, insufficient attention has been devoted to poems that describe sculptures or deal with sculpturing. Such poems, when identified, will constitute a body of literature to which the generic designation "sculptural poetry" may be applied. The arc that encompasses sculptural poetry extends through many eras and across numerous authors. If in order to develop a prolegomenon to a theory of genre one were to select three writers, then Michelangelo, Keats, and Shelley will serve as points of reference. The foregoing authors, while referring to visual artifacts or to the process by which they are conceived and created, explore not only the act of creativity but also the art of interpretation. ⟨...⟩

The interdependence of sculpture and poetry, for which Michelangelo provides a frame of reference and point of departure, encourages inquiry into the sculptural poetry of other authors. If we limit discussion to one era, then in nineteenth-century England the following two works, among other examples, may be cited: John Keats's "Ode on a Grecian Urn" and Percy Bysshe Shelley's "Ozymandias." ⟨...⟩

Interpreting Shelley's "Ozymandias" as sculptural poetry enhances our understanding of the sonnet while enriching our awareness of the tradition⌊ The poem is the speaker's verbatim account of what "a traveller from an antique land" told him after having seen the ruins of a grandiose sculpture, the likeness of Ozymandias, a proud king. Using two speakers, distant and immediate, or a listener-turned-narrator enables Shelley to enlarge distance and expand time. The statue of Ozymandias was not seen by the immediate narrator, though the distant narrator did view it or, to be precise, its ruins. The sculptor who created the likeness saw and studied the living Ozymandias. Carved on the pedestal is sculptural poetry, a distich: "My name is Ozymandias, king of kings: / Look on my works, ye Mighty, and despair!" Whether the sculptor composed, as well as carved, the distich is uncertain. He may have simply inscribed what the living king himself dictated. In this way the sculpture while erect and intact was animated by the king's own words. If, however, the artist versified about, indeed *on*, the statue, then his poetry, like Michelangelo's, not only adds psychic and emotional life to the statue but also accentuates the character and personality already conveyed by the visual likeness of the king:

> Half sunk, a shattered visage lies, whose frown,
> And wrinkled lip, and sneer of cold command,
> Tell that its sculptor well those passions read
> Which yet survive, stamped on these lifeless things,
> The hand that mocked them, and the heart that fed.

While describing the sculpture as a visual medium, the foregoing passage by its use of *tell* and *read* also alludes to oral and written communication, respectively. Beyond means of expression, the same passage simultaneously refers to modes of interpretation. Thus the sculptor who saw the living Ozymandias interpreted or "read" the king's imperiousness, and through the statue that he carved and the distich that he inscribed, if not composed, he seeks to "tell" or express what he "read." The distant narrator then "reads" or views both the ruins of the sculpture and the inscription on the pedestal. He "tells," in turn, the immediate narrator, who, having seen neither the sculpture nor the distich, "tells" what has been recounted and "read" to him.

Across space and through time, the sculpture, its ruins, and the distich inspire many tellings and elicit numerous readings. The resulting ironies and ambiguities enable the reader of the sonnet not only to animate the sculpture but also to enliven the artist. One speculates on the grandeur of a past civilization and the arrogance of its king, as well as on the pretentiousness of the monumental statue and the possible vainglory of its sculptor. One conjectures whether the sculptor may not have been victimized by the same passions that beset Ozymandias. If the arrogance embodied in Ozymandias were likewise embedded in the sculptor's heart, to which rasp and chisel were applied in self-sculpturing, then the monument is also a projection of its maker. Accordingly, "the hand that *mocked*" (emphasis mine) the passions represents *imitatively* or "tells" through art not only what the sculptor "read" in the living king but also what was *mimetically* and *repetitively* experienced within himself. When the statue is perceived as a metonymy of the civilization, the "heart that fed" the passions refers to the king and the sculptor, both of whom collaborated in a monument of vanity that has become a memorial to folly, for which the distich is finally a *mocking* or derisive epitaph after having been an arrogant proclamation. Were the sculptor unaffected by the monarch's passions, then his "hand that mocked them" in art may have been guided by a prescient outlook, foreseeing the inevitable decline and fall of a tyrant, a civilization, and its monuments. In this way the sculptor comments *mockingly* on vainglorious aspirations—whether imperialistic or artistic. The remains of Ozymandias, aptly described as a "colossal wreck," further suggest that the nearly extinguished civilization will soon become extinct, like that for which the Colossus of Rhodes was the monument. Even its ruins no longer exist. What may one reckon—or "read"—in such *mocking* losses, imitated and repeated in many places and at different times? What may one "tell" about them?

—Albert C. Labriola, "Sculptural Poetry: The Visual Imagination of Michelangelo, Keats, and Shelley," *Comparative Literature Studies* 24, no. 4 (1987): pp. 326, 330–33.

WILLIAM FREEDMAN ON MULTIPLE IDENTITIES OF THE NARRATIVE VOICE

[William Freedman is the author of "The Monster in Plath's 'Mirror'" (1993) and "The Literary Motif: A Definition and Evaluation" (1996). In the excerpt below from his article, "Postponement and Perspectives in Shelley's 'Ozymandias,'" Freedman discusses the complex relationship amongst the multiple identities of the narrative voice and the problem of knowledge within the poem.]

Probably few poems are at once as widely known and little discussed as Shelley's "Ozymandias." ⟨. . .⟩

What little study the poem has stimulated has been devoted chiefly to the quest for sources, predictably in the accounts of traveler-historians, for Shelley's powerful description of the shattered statue and its suggestive inscription. The original statue, it seems likely, is that described by Diodorus Siculus in his *Bibliotheca Historica* (first century B.C.). Diodorus praises a massive sitting statue of a Pharaoh (identifiably Ramses II) "admirable for its art and workmanship, and the excellency of its stone" and bearing the inscription: "I am Osymandias, king of kings; if any would know how great I am, and where I lie, let him excel me in any of my works." ⟨. . .⟩

In the case of "Ozymandias," background inquires into the identity of Shelley's traveler and statue bring us closer to the literary experience of the poem than almost all the dismissively brief assurances about its theme. The concern of "Ozymandias" scholarship is the search for origins and sources, for the multiply filtered relationships between Ozymandias (or Ramses II), the sculptor (probably Memnon of Sienitas) who rendered his gigantic form at the Pharaoh's behest, the many traveler-historians who described, with varying degrees of precision and reliability, the statues they saw or learned of, and the poet Shelley. That, I will contend, complicated still further by the inevitable addition of the reader of the poem, is also the subject, at least *a* subject, of Shelley's poem. Searches for the stone and paper origins of "Ozymandias" are scholarly accounts of a poet's rendering of a historian's report of a sculptor's time-altered fashioning of a tyrant and his vain boast. Critical readings of the poem are, for literary rather than historical reasons, reflections of that many-lensed gaze. They are interpretations of the poet's (apparently ironic) judgment of a tale allegedly told him by a traveler recollecting his impressions of an artist's time- and fate-shattered rendering of a historical figure's visage and character and his inscription of that ruler's own assessment of the magnitude, prospects, and implications of his achievements.

Serious efforts to come to terms with "Ozymandias" are a rarity, but none can take place without some reference to the curious presence of the filtering "traveller from an antique land." Why interpose him? Why does the speaker or poet not describe directly the fallen statue he has seen or sees? One answer, by far the most familiar, is that the traveler, "a reliable fellow," in Desmond King-Hele's urbane judgment, "quick to observe relevant detail and not too wild in interpreting it," lends credibility to the poem's report. Another, less often heard but feasible, is that by displacing the testimony from first to second hand, Shelley introduces what otherwise would hardly occur to us: the possibility of doubting its validity. For while the removal depersonalizes the account in a way Shelley, that preeminently personal poet, apparently found intriguing, voices other than the poet's or those that pass for his are almost inevitably less automatically credited than his own. This question, however, like the issues of sources, is ultimately more interesting as a reflection of the questions and issues the poem itself raises and vies with than for the answers either gives. For what is quite undeniable is that—whether at the price or added profit of credibility—the poet "distances himself from the poem's subject by having all details supplied by some unnamed traveler." ⟨...⟩

The implication of the poem's ironic comment on the transience of human power and accomplishment is that the truth is not, as

Ozymandias and perhaps the sculptor believed, the product of first perception; one must wait for reliable or final answers. Almost everything in "Ozymandias" supports and enriches this notion, complicating it finally to the point where even that seemingly reliable inference forfeits, like the statue, its solidity.

The apparent meaning of the poem is itself postponed until the last lines, even a bit beyond their reading to the delayed grasp of the ironic disharmony between the inscribed boast and the leveling sands that follow and erode it. Not until we arrive at the closing words of the poem and perhaps beyond them do we realize that process is point, that knowledge is a matter of postponement and delayed recognition.

—William Freedman, "Postponement and Perspectives in Shelley's 'Ozymandias,'" *Studies in Romanticism* 25, no. 1 (Spring 1986): pp. 63–66.

KELVIN EVEREST ON THE TRAVELER'S DILEMMA

[Kelvin Everest is an editor of *Percy Bysshe Shelley: Bicentenary Essays* (1992) and *Reflections of Revolution: Images of Romanticism* (1993). In the excerpt below, Everest discusses the structure of the poem, which he sees as moving from an initially direct statement to an interpretive and ambivalent dilemma as the traveler strives to elicit meaning from a monument in ruins.]

I want in this essay to explore a number of questions raised by recent broad trends in literary theory. These trends are towards an emphasis on creativity and freedom in the act of interpretation. The drive is to dispense with the idea of the 'Author' and of authorial intention—authority—and to stress instead the liberated polysemic and many-voiced character of criticism. The sources and elaborations of critical positions of this kind are nowadays very well-known, and need no new rehearsal here. They call into question the status of the text which is the occasion for criticism, by implying that meaning resides more or less exclusively in the interpreting consciousness and its contexts. A refinement of this view has more recently drawn upon developments in the theory of textual criticism strictly conceived—that is, the theory of the editing of texts—to argue that texts materially mutate, inevitably, in the ordinary processes by which they are transmitted through time. ⟨. . .⟩

Shelley's sonnet 'Ozymandias' is undoubtedly amongst the best-known of all his poems. Since the mid-nineteenth century it has been anthologised countless times. Even nowadays, when the place of pre-twentieth century English poetry in any really existent shared national culture is clearly reduced, there is a good chance that most educated people will at least have come across the poem. ⟨. . .⟩

It has, so to speak, survived; its persists beyond the immediate context of its making, like a monument fixed in a setting which has long since changed out of all recognition.

It is puzzling that the sonnet has attracted very little attention from Shelley's commentators. Perhaps it is considered too obvious, or too brief; perhaps it even seems rather uncharacteristic of Shelley's typical styles and habits of mind. But its strategies, even if on the face of it too obvious for comment, will perhaps emerge as more complicated and elusive in the process of being spelt out. It is however first necessary, as a part of the argument I wish to develop, to establish the form of the poem which my critical analysis will address. It is a hybrid form, created by an editor (the present writer). ⟨. . .⟩

It's a simple moral. The tyrant's affirmation of his omnipotence, sneeringly arrogant and contemptuous of its human cost, has been ironised by time. The scene reported by the traveller gives the lie unanswerably to the boast on the pedestal; more than that, the scene most tellingly inverts the claims of the legend, 'Look on my Works ye Mighty, and despair!' Ozymandias's message to posterity has ended up articulating just exactly the opposite to what was intended.

The poem's grammatical construction subtly reinforces this most emphatic of the poem's first impressions, the unanswerable quality of its irony. We feel that the question of tyranny's durability and the validity of its claims to universal power has been settled absolutely by what we learn, taken completely beyond argument and debate. It is simply true that tyranny does not last. The poem's air of dispassionately reporting a simple truth is an effect, in part at least, of the measured and deliberated movement of the verse. The syntax is, in the first few lines, entirely that of careful speech, both in the opening line or so which the poet speaks, and in the studied observations that the traveller conveys. The marked grammatical pause at the end of the first line, emphasised with a comma, lends a kind of conviction and definiteness to the 'Who said' at the beginning of line two; we are inclined to believe the poet's reporting of what the traveller reports, as well as the report itself. The provenance is made to seem reliable. The traveller's own words are shaped into a syntactical and grammatical sequence which dramatises a careful, almost itemised procedure of surveying and noting, distantly suggesting the style of British Levantine topographical and early archaeological writings. ⟨...⟩

The believable directness of tone, with its implication that the details of the scene are being specified in a verifiable way, is superseded in lines 6–8 by a more difficult syntactic organisation, as the traveller's account moves away from the descriptive manner and into an interpretational idiom. Here we're made to feel the different and more taxing intellectual demands of teasing a meaning from the monument. There is room now, even a need, for a way of speaking which suits ambivalence and difficulty. The sculpted face has features which suggest to the traveller that its maker had accurately interpreted the generic characteristics of the Tyrant. This prompts a further reflection on the way that the representation of Ozymandias's 'visage' has long outlasted both the living human who nourished tyrannical qualities in his person and conduct, and the living artist who effected the representation (the pronoun 'them' in line eight of course refers to the 'passions' of line six, and this same pronoun is then understood after 'fed'). This is in fact not quite the same irony which we have so far been noting in the sonnet. It is now not simply that Ozymandias's claim to omnipotence has been invalidated by its lone survival in a setting otherwise utterly changed; this irony is compounded and complicated by the additional fact that what has really survived is the artist's skill in representation and interpretation.

—Kelvin Everest, "'Ozymandias': The Text in Time," *Essays and Studies* 45 (1992): pp. 24–28.

Desmond King-Hele on the Ravages of Time in the Poem

[Desmond King-Hele is the author of *Doctor of Revolution: The Life and Genius of Erasmus Darwin* (1977) and *Erasmus Darwin and the Romantic Poets* (1986). In the excerpt below from his book, King-Hele discusses "Ozymandias" in terms of both the ravages of time and Shelley's ironic use of the "lure" of the traveler's tale.]

Few of Shelley's sonnets can bear comparison with Shakespeare's, but in *Ozymandias* he successfully challenges the master on his favourite ground, the ravages of time. Shelley seems here to wriggle out of the fetters of the sonnet form, flouting the rules with narrative, doubly reported speech, and a curious rhyme-scheme. He is justified by the result, one of those rare poems which can, on occasion, please even a poetry-hater. ⟨...⟩

In *The Revolt of Islam* we were bludgeoned; here the detached tone lulls our suspicions and the irony appeals to our vanity. The first ten words of the poem, though standing apart, contribute to the effect, for in them Shelley exploits the age-old lure of travellers' tales and at the same time implies he himself will merely report, not interpret, what the traveller has to say. The tale begins well, with a series of arresting visual images. Then we have the deliberate diminuendo of the lines about the sculptor, with the involved grammar, the gentle speculation and the archaic *mocked* (for *mimicked*) creating an olde-worlde air. We are by now persuaded that the traveller is a reliable fellow, quick to observe relevant detail and not too wild in interpreting it. The quiet interval also lets us recover from the poem's first impact and focus our attention on the simple *fortissimo* statements to follow. The crux of the poem is the inscription on the pedestal, and this is far removed from any hint of bias, because it is the veracious traveller's report of what someone else wrote. The last three lines of the poem, flat and direct, seem innocent enough, yet they have a compelling finality. How is this achieved? There is the music of the verse, the satisfying sequence of vowels and the deft alliteration. There is *nothing beside remains*, a sentence which is the richer for seeming to include, as an undercurrent, 'no other remains exist near by.' Finally, there is the orator's trick of repetition, artfully disguised: 'sand, bare, level and boundless, surrounds that colossal wreck' conveys the meaning in nine words instead of eighteen, but the air of finality, as well as the music, has been lost.

The poem subtly flatters our vanity. We feel after reading it that we are wiser than Ozymandias, who never knew the irony of his inscription, and wiser too than the traveller, who seems unaware of any moral to be drawn from his plain tale. A real traveller's tale does lie in the background, for *Ozymandias*, like *Kubla Khan* and the ballad of *The Revenge*, is one of those poems which can clearly be tracked to a prose source. Ozymandias was one of the Greek names for Rameses II, and the first of the two key lines in the poem paraphrases an inscription on an Egyptian temple recorded by Diodorus Siculus, 'I am Ozymandias, king of kings.' The traveller may have been Dr. Pococke, who described such statues in 1743.

No one who was asked to select a typical poem of Shelley's would choose *Ozymandias*: intuitively one feels the poem is completely *un*typical, and it is not difficult to see why. First there is the subject: Shelley usually wrote about things dear to his heart, while Ozymandias is a little remote. Then there is the tone, which, partly because of the subject, is passionless, objective and calm, instead of being passionate, subjective and excited. Last, and perhaps most important, there is the aim. Shelley's habit was to aim high, sometimes impossibly high, and even though he would often turn out that most rewarding type of poem which yields new layers of meaning at each re-reading, his success was rarely complete. In *Ozymandias*, however, he is content with a limited objective, a straightforward piece of irony, and he succeeds completely.

—Desmond King-Hele, *Shelley: His Thought and Work* (Cranbury, New Jersey: Associated University Presses, 1984): pp. 92–94.

Thematic Analysis of
"To a Skylark"

Written in late June 1820 and published in the *Prometheus Unbound* volume in the same year, "To a Skylark" is a lyric (a poem which is both musical and expressive in origin, and which focuses on the poet's emotional responses to the world outside the self and his relationship to that world). The poet addresses the skylark, a small European bird that sings only while in flight, usually only when too high to be visible to human eyes; this fact has important implications later in the poem. As Desmond King-Hele has pointed out, addressing a skylark is a fiction, and that fiction is based on the notion of a conceit (a complex, implied comparison in which a poet juxtaposes images or ideas that seemingly have no real correspondence but which serve to make an important and memorable statement). The conceit in this poem is the skylark, a creature whose description dominates the entire poem, with whom the poet seeks to communicate.

Thematically, "To a Skylark" contains three distinct parts: lines 1–30 describing the flight of the skylark, lines 31–60 in which the poet attempts to find a fitting analogue for the bird and its song, and lines 61–105 in which the poet asks the bird to teach humanity about its secret joy.

In the first line, the poet greets the carefree bird as a "blithe Spirit," and a little further on, we recognize that Shelley has rhetorically transformed his skylark into a creature that neither belongs to this world nor is identifiable as such: "Bird thou never wert." Instead, Shelley's skylark is a celestial visitor, "from Heaven, or near it," whose sole purpose is to celebrate its joyful heart, "in profuse strains of unpremeditated art," a being capable of an original and spontaneous creativity we will eventually understand as an expression of the poet's own desires. The result of Shelley's "transformation" of his skylark into a purely spiritual being is that his beloved bird will move farther and father away from both his vision and his grasp: "Higher still and higher / From the earth thou springest." Indeed, the less accessible the skylark becomes, the more we come to realize that this poem is about the poet's longing to possess the same poetic powers Shelley has bestowed upon his celestial bird.

The second stanza ends with an important rhetorical device known as *chiasmus*. "And singing still dost soar, and soaring ever singest." Chiasmus, named for the Greek letter X ("chi") means "a placing crosswise," a sentence consisting of two main clauses, the first clause being an exact reversal of the second, while still retaining the same meaning. In "To a Skylark," this rhetorical device functions as a mirror image of the poet's desire to identify with the lark, a desire we will eventually understand must remain unfulfilled. Shelley's skylark is pure spirit, "an unbodied joy," which sings beautifully while becoming evermore distant. This spirit will ultimately require a leap of faith in order for the poet to confirm its very existence: "Whose intense lamp narrows / In the white dawn clear / Until we hardly see—we feel that it is there." As the skylark vanishes, it becomes increasingly difficult for Shelley to describe the object of his desire in human terms, as will be illustrated several times in the second section of the poem. In other words, language itself will become an obstacle for defining his "imaginary" skylark.

This same language problem, in which Shelley seeks to find a more realistic way to describe his highly idealized skylark, is heightened in the second section of the poem. The first stanza of this section begins by posing the critical question the poet will find increasingly difficult to answer: "What thou art we know not; / What is most like thee? / From rainbow clouds there flow not / Drops so bright to see." What follows is a series of attempts to find an earthly comparison. This manifests two important patterns: First, the natural phenomena through which Shelley strives to understand the truth about his imaginary skylark moves downward through the hierarchy of earthy existence, beginning with the highest order to which the Poet belongs, "hidden / In the light of thought," down through the animal world of "a glow-worm golden," to the vegetable and mineral forms of life represented by roses and vernal showers. Second, in almost every instance, Shelley's ability to compare his skylark to anyone or anything recognizable utterly fails, for in each instance, the man is not yet ready to know or receive the spiritual message that remains hidden from the mundane powers of the senses. The Poet singing his hymns is "unbidden" and, although his musical powers come from an unearthly realm, we also sense he is an uninvited guest, waiting "[t]ill the world is wrought / To sympathy." Neither does the comparison work with the "high-born maiden" of the following stanza, for she is a figure imprisoned in "a palace-tower," plucked from a medieval romance, a fictitious being existing only in the courtly love tradition of unrequited love, "[s]oothing her love-laden / Soul in secret hour." As of the "glowworm," a very rudimentary example of the animal world, the light he is able to bestow is sadly and wholly-unrecognized, a "[s]cattering unbeholden / Its aerial hue / Among the flowers and grass which screen it from the view." And, finally, the rose is hidden from view, "embowered / In its own green leaves," whose scent once stolen by the warm winds, is wasted, and "[m]akes faint with too much sweet these heavy-winged thieves."

By the time we reach the third and final section of the poem, the poet has failed to find in the physical world any likeness to the skylark. He is still unsure of what to make of a creature who is beyond the descriptive powers of human language, and so he beseeches his beloved bird to instruct him. "Teach us, Sprite or Bird, / What sweet thoughts are thine; / I have never heard / Praise of love or wine / That panted forth a flood of rapture so divine." The supreme and magical powers of Greek mythological beings pale in comparison: "Chorus Hymeneal / Or triumphal chaunt / Matched with thine would be all / But an empty vaunt."

Shelley's choice of mythic analogue, the hymeneal, is a deliberate one and serves two functions. First, it refers to both Hymen, the Greek god of marriage, as well as to the hymenaeus—the traditional wedding song or processional that accompanied the newly married couple to their home. Second, and more important, these lines express an implicit desire, namely that the poet wishes to be united with the skylark's creative powers, "[a] thing wherein we feel there is some hidden want" and at the same time, to exist alongside the skylark in a spiritual world, far from the vicissitudes of earthly passion, a place where love is "keen joyance." "Thou lovest—but ne'er knew love's sad satiety."

However, the poet recognizes that he still lives in the physical world of mortality and longing. This same "tragic" condition of human life produces great poetry. "Our sweetest songs are those that tell of saddest thought." And so the poem ends with the poet trying to effect a compromise, imploring his skylark to grant him half its powers so humanity will hear the poet's inspired message: "Teach me half the gladness / That thy brain must know, / . . . The world should listen then—as I am listening now." ❈

Critical Views on
"To a Skylark"

WILLIAM A. ULMER ON THE CONTRARY NATURE OF "JOY"

[William A. Ulmer is the author of *Shelleyan Eros: The Rhetoric of Romantic Love* (1990). In the excerpt below, Ulmer discusses contrary nature of "joy" within the poem, a joy that vacillates between a "dream of limitless bliss" and the human "experience of mundane limitation."]

"To a Sky-Lark" celebrates a joy so exhilarating it seems a harbinger of the Eternal and One, higher realities Shelley believed accessible to the imagination. So at least it has seemed to innumerable critics. The final wisdom of "Sky-Lark" rests not on transcendent assurances, however, nor on the possibility of a "wholly unalloyed" delight, but on Shelley's contrary awareness that "from an inexplicable defect of harmony in the constitution of human nature, the pain of the inferior is frequently connected with the pleasures of the superior portions of our being." This awareness exerts an antiphonal pressure on Shelley's poem, subtly complicating its affirmations. Far less blithe and unreflecting than it may at first appear, "Sky-Lark" in fact demonstrates the impossibility of either gratifying infinite desire or renouncing it. The poem finally attributes this impossibility to the inherent contrariety of language and imagination. Addressing the psychological dynamics of aspiration, Shelley shows the dream of limitless bliss to be a belated projection of human desire, a projection born of and indelibly shaped by the experience of mundane limitation, without which such dreams could not exist. But since Shelley establishes sadness as the necessary condition for joy, concern with the sadness of "To a Sky-Lark" does not make it a less joyous poem—merely one which interrogates the elation it renders with such wonder and spontaneity.

The elation is of course Shelley's response to an irresistible invitation. Although the bird's music has only freed feelings already latent in the speaker, it initially seems not merely the occasion for the ecstasy but the potentially reclaimable source of it. In fact, perhaps the definitive characteristic of the lark's song is its power of instantly prompting a lyrical human response: this is seemingly inspiration incarnate. From the first greeting he utters, Shelley's persona invokes the elusive, singing lark as the origin of his own song. Consequently, when Shelley portrayed the imagination as belated in his famous comparison of "the mind in creation" to a dying coal, and so tacitly defined the creative enterprise as an orchestration of vestiges, a quest for an elusive, fading origin, he described precisely the basic situation of "To a Sky-Lark," and perhaps of many poems. "Since poetry . . . does not go back to a truly divine origin," Harold Bloom generalizes, "poetry is always at work *imagining its own origin*, or telling a persuasive lie about itself, to itself." For Bloom, a poem is a lie against time which tries to circumvent its own inherent belatedness by internalizing the origin in an act of revisionary appropriation. For Shelley in "Sky-Lark," the belatedness of poetic expression will remain just part of the problem. As the speaker searches for comparisons that can convey both his rapture and the bird's beauty, he seeks an incarnating language that can subserve an identity of self and origin. Yet his comparisons never effect such identity. The lark remains both like and unlike every object he offers, so that these various offerings finally show that dissimilarity is actually the necessary precondition of any comparison. Clarifying the differential premises and structure of metaphor, as a vehicle for imaginative perception, "Sky-Lark" works to foreground correlatively the differential structure of human thought and emotion.

It is Shelley's concern with this structure that gives the poem its importance, its centrality both to the tradition of the ode and to his own career. As "To a Sky-Lark" eventually abandons the search for a transcendent power of language, it confesses to the same "burden of doubt" that Paul Fry finds in all English odes, but which both the progress of history and Shelley's own skeptical allegiances worked to intensify. However intrinsic the problems of any vocative mode, they certainly increased with that deepening of artistic self-consciousness so characteristic of romanticism. ⟨. . .⟩

"Sky-Lark" was written during one of the bleakest periods of the poet's life, the first half of 1820. The poem consequently stands between the apocalyptic optimism of *Prometheus Unbound* and the darkened mood of *The Triumph of Life*, and, for all its joyous spontaneity, testifies to that gradual darkening. The spontaneity even becomes an obstacle to poetic incarnation at last. ⟨. . .⟩

The tonal immediacy of "To a Sky-Lark," as Shelley actually hears a ringing heavenly music, makes this saving conversion unavailable until the end, and forces him to confront the differential matrix and inherent contradiction of any vision of the One.

—William A. Ulmer, "Some Hidden Want: Aspiration in 'To a Sky-Lark,'" *Studies in Romanticism* 23, no. 2 (Summer 1984): pp. 245–48.

PARKS C. HUNTER JR. ON THE UNIVERSAL IDEAS WITHIN CLASSICAL FORMS

[Parks C. Hunter Jr. is the author of *Textual Differences in the Drafts of Shelley's "Una Favola"* (1966). In the excerpt below, Hunter discusses "To a Skylark" in terms of Shelley's interest in the *Anacreontea* (a collection of ancient Greek lyric poems chiefly interested in wine and love), an interest motivated by Shelley's pursuit of universal ideas to be found in classical forms.]

Anacreontics began to influence English poetry with the French scholar Henri Estienne's discovery and publication in 1554 of the *Anacreontea* and with the efforts of the Pleiade, the first to translate and adapt the odes and thus to provide the threads of which many Elizabethan lyrics were woven. Not only did the Anacreontics continue popular in the days of Abraham Cowley and Thomas Stanley, but they have gone on repeating themselves in every generation of our poets; and in Shelley's generation all of the major poets were to some extent familiar with the Anacreontics.

K. Jerome Wilkinson has remarked:

> The Greek poet celebrated wine, women, and singing and dancing as necessary elements in a joyful, lusty life. We get the impression from reading the original that these joys are somehow ritualistic. This point of view resulted in a tone which was light, joyful, sometimes orgiastic, but never obscene and ribald.

What would seem more natural than for the popular, joyous, archetypal Anacreontic odes to attract Shelley, England's greatest lyric poet? For despite the effects of spontaneity and originality that his lyrics produce, "Shelley at his maturity rarely expressed outward forms without allusion to some universal and permanent idea," and "no other poet has approached Shelley's magical deceptions." Indeed, Shelley's philosophy of poetry, his method of composition, and the nature of "To a Skylark" and "The Cloud" as vehicles of reform suggest classical models. As Gilbert Highet points out:

> . . . when lyric poetry grows less private and more reflective, then it can and often does enrich itself by subtilizations of thought, elaborations of pattern, new devices of style and imagery, adapted from Greco-Roman lyric and fused into a new alloy.

Before we may consider the influence of two particular Anacreontic odes, "To the Cicada" and "Drinking," upon "To a Skylark" and "The Cloud," we must prove that a significantly important relationship between Anacreon and Shelley did exist. First, while at Oxford, Shelley translated selections from the *Greek Anthology*, that contained some Anacreon. Second, by 1820, when "To a Skylark" and "The Cloud" appeared, Shelley was proficient enough in Greek to have translated the Anacreontics from the original. And third, Shelley's letters of November 3, 1819 to Leigh Hunt and of c. May 21, 1822 to Horace Smith mention Anacreon. ⟨. . .⟩

With "To a Skylark" to be considered first, Shelley's transposition of cicada (grasshopper) to lark should not disturb us. Significantly, previous bird poems "do not seem to have deeply influenced Shelley" (Stewart C. Wilcox). Although the Greeks did recognize the lark, Shelley would not have found the lark venerated in Greek lyrics. Since the ancients seem never to have thought of eulogizing the lark, whose song did not appeal to them, he could not have drawn upon a Greek skylark lyric for the archetypal ideas reflected in "To a Skylark." On the other hand, the cicada did hold much the same position for the Greeks as the lark now holds in English poetry, and the Greeks ascribed to the nightingale traits that modern poetry now reserves for the skylark. Thus, in two poems contemporaneous with "To a Skylark" (*Oedipus Tyrannus*, I, ll. 39-42, and "The Witch of Atlas," viii, ll. 1-4) Shelley mentions the grasshopper and cicada in contexts suggesting his knowledge of the Greek esteem for the insects.

As second in importance to Shelley's transposition of cicada to lark, disembodiment links the skylark with the Anacreontic cicada, their voices raining down on mankind from an undiscoverable source. To reinforce this common bond of the rapturous singing, the ideal being transcending experience, and the unseen power, Shelley says: "Thou art unseen, but yet I hear thy shrill delight." Bearing significantly upon the undiscoverable source idea, all of the images from Shelley's series of similes—"like a poet hidden," "like a high-born maiden," "like a glowworm golden," "like a rose embower'd"—have one idea in common, that of concealment.

Third in importance, what attracts our attention is that each little disembodied, hidden creature epitomizes joy *par excellence* and that Shelley has captured the same transcendence of the physical that the translations do. Instead of allowing the corporeality of the subject ever to become important, Shelley using the skylark and the translators using the cicada concentrate upon "the divine, superrational quality of poetry." This disembodied character of the cicada mentioned in the concluding lines of each translation occurs in ll. 14-5 of "To a Skylark," with the peculiar "unbodied" as an exact echo from the last line of Elton's translation.

Fourth, in addition to the common strain of disembodied joy that connects "To a Skylark" with "To the Cicada," Shelley has also chosen to develop in the last third of "To a Skylark" (chiefly in ll. 81-5) the complementary strain of victory over death appearing in "To the Cicada" and described in the concluding lines of all of the translations.

—Parks C. Hunter Jr., "Undercurrents of Anacreontics in Shelley's 'To a Skylark' and 'The Cloud,'" *Studies in Philology* 65, no. 4 (July 1968): pp. 677–79, 683–84.

DIANA HENDRY ON THE UNCERTAINTY OF SHELLEY'S "BODILESS BIRD"

[In the excerpt below from her article, Diana Hendry discusses "To a Skylark" as Shelley's conversation with Wordsworth's "Skylark," finding a greater uncertainty in Shelley's skylark, a bird "famously bodiless."]

Skylarks haven't been the same since Ted Hughes. For readers of the future, Shelley's 'blithe spirit' and Wordsworth's 'pilgrim of the skies' will have faded into the ozone layer, their symbolic associations with dawn and hope, joy and inspiration, lost forever. Hughes's bird, a creature 'Crueller than owl or eagle' will reign supreme.

Children (if skylarks aren't extinct) will not think of them singing 'at heaven's gate' but 'Scrambling/ In a nightmare difficulty/ Up through the nothing.' It is all very sad. It is also a very simple way of comparing how poets of the nineteenth and twentieth century think about poets and poetry. You want the ideology? Consider skylarks.

In particular consider Shelley's 'To a Skylark' (1820), Wordsworth's poem of the same title (1825) and Hughes's 'Skylarks' (1967). Perhaps, for good measure (or the last of hopefulness) one should add Isaac Rosenberg's 'Returning, We Hear the Larks' (1917). Skylarks, in this poem, could be said to be on the turn between centuries. No post-war lark could sing, like Shelley's, 'of rapture so divine,' or, when the airways are so crowded, enjoy, like Wordsworth's lark 'a privacy of glorious light.'

In Rosenbergs's poem 'Death could drop from the dark/ As easily as song' and the sweetness of the larks' song is somehow suspect. It is compared to a girl's kisses 'where a serpent hides.' That it should be song, rather than death, dropping from the skies represents not pure joy but pure chance.

All four poems seem to be part of a conversation between poets. There are points on which Shelley and Wordsworth are in agreement. For both poets the skylark represents divine inspiration. Their larks are mystics pouring upon the world a 'flood/ Of harmony' (Wordsworth) or 'Singing hymns unbidden,/ Till the world is wrought/ To sympathy with hopes and fears it heeded not:' (Shelley).

Shelley's lark, famously bodiless, is all 'blithe spirit'; Wordsworth's an 'Ethereal minstrel' and, though it keeps an eye on its earthly nest, we are given no physical description of the bird. No 'shadow of annoyance' ever came near Shelley's lark. It has no knowledge of pain; it knows love but not 'love's sad satiety'; it knows death but also something about death 'more true and deep/ Than we mortals dream.' It is all gladness and 'harmonious madness.'

One can imagine Wordsworth, firmly earthed in the Lake District, reading Shelley's poem and saying 'now, steady up a bit.' For while Shelley seems to imply that the skylark scorns 'Hate, and pride and fear' (and, by implication, all worldly matters), Wordsworth, asking his lark the rhetorical question 'Dost thou despise the earth where cares abound?' comes back with a clear 'no.' Even while the skylark's wings 'aspire,' its 'heart and eye' are both with its nest 'upon the dewy ground.' Indeed the last lines of the poem could well contain a moral message directed expressly at Shelley.

> Type of the wise who soar, but never roam;
> True to the kindred points of Heaven and Home!

> —Diana Hendry, "Up with the Lark(s)," *Critical Survey* 4, no. 1 (1992): pp. 67–68.

NICHOLAS MEIHUIZEN ON THE SYMPATHETIC RELATIONSHIP BETWEEN HUMANITY AND BIRDS

[Nicholas Meihuizen is the author of *Yeats and the Drama of Sacred Space* (1998). In the excerpt below from his article, "'Birds and Bird-Song in Wordsworth, Shelley and Yeats: The Study of a Relationship Between Three Poems," Meihuizen discusses the relationship between humans and birds, a relationship marked simultaneously by the pleasure of bird singing and its link to expressions of pain born of an awareness of human limitations.]

If bird-song is closely linked to the song of man in "The Solitary Reaper," the opposite is true in Shelley's "To a Skylark," which tells of a joyfulness beyond man's experience apparent in the song of this bird. A string of comparisons drawn from many aspects of nature's excellence both serves to place the bird-song at its proper level, and, compounded, indicates its superiority; the comparisons end with a clear acknowledgement of this superiority: "All that ever was/ Joyous, and clear, and fresh, thy music doth surpass."

As with Wordsworth and his reaper, Shelley also desires to understand the import of the song, although not for the sake of simple interpretation or sympathetic curiosity; more intensely (and more characteristically) he wants to learn from it: "Teach us, Sprite or Bird,/ What sweet thoughts are thine."

The song is then compared with human song, and, as opposed to Wordsworth's vision, found infinitely superior. "Praise of love or wine," "Chorus Hymeneal" and "triumphal chant" are all found wanting in comparison. "What objects are the fountains/ Of thy happy strain?" parallels Wordsworth's "Will no one tell me what she sings?" and contains come instructive differences. Shelley is in direct communion with the bird, Wordsworth appeals to a third party; for Wordsworth the meaning is joined to inescapable, sad events, for Shelley, the notes are "happy." The evidence suggests Wordsworth's distance from the song, and Shelley's proximity to it. These emphases are rooted in the poems, and are indicative of the two poets' different approaches to their art at present: for Shelley the emphasis is on the "unpremeditated" outpouring, virtually unprocessed; for Wordsworth the emphasis is on a "spontaneous overflow" indeed, but processed in a meditative manner, given to the indirect technique of asking rhetorical questions. The evidence, on the face of it, also suggests Shelley's idealistic optimism, and Wordsworth's bleaker fatalism. But Shelleyan optimism is tinged by an awareness of the inadequacy of human life, which the bird-song defines:

> Yet if we could scorn
> > Hate, and pride, and fear;
> If we were things born
> > Not to shed a tear,
> I know not how thy joy we ever should come near.

(There is another way of interpreting these lines: Our human limitations enable us to "come near" the "joy" of the bird. And yet our "Hate, and pride, and fear" still define our inadequacy.) By contrast Wordsworthian fatalism is conditioned by the deep emotional and physical pleasure imparted by his song. Both men were solitaries in their own way, but Shelley's bright idealism is touched by a dissatisfaction which cannot be imputed to Wordsworth. Man and his experience are very obviously the centre of Wordsworth's relationship with nature, for Shelley man always falls short, as indicated above.

—Nicholas Meihuizen, "Birds and Bird-Song in Wordsworth, Shelley, and Yeats: The Study of a Relationship Between Three Poems," *English Studies in Africa* 31, no. 1 (Winter 1988): pp. 55–58.

Nathan Cervo on Spirit and Matter

[Nathan Cervo is the author of "Webster's White Devil" (1988) and "The Dangerous Conflict Between Nature and Grace in Hopkins's Poetry" (1993). In the excerpt below from his article, "Hopkins's *The Caged Skylark* and Shelley's *To a Skylark*," Cervo discusses Shelley's attempt to reconcile spirit and matter.]

First of all, by way of preamble, it should be noted that Hopkins does not split reality into two opposing, utterly irreconcilable factions, with *spirit* construed as hostile or indifferent to *matter* and doctrinairely, by extrapolation or simple inference, to matter's specious, irrelevant claims. For Hopkins, morality is the discipline of matter. (Since the Greek word for discipline is *ascesis*, it is possible to speak of Hopkins's ascetic attitude toward nature, by which nothing more should be meant or understood than his piety, rigorous as it is.) Bizarrely enough, it is the humanitarian-pantheist Percy Bysshe Shelley who seems to fall between these two stools (spirit and matter) by attempting to effectuate an inane peace treaty between them by treating them as modes of a single transcendental, yet paradoxically always immanent, entity, with change viewed solely as the necessary ontological exhalation of that entity. Under such conditions, the epistemology requisite to response within Shelley's monistic system is circular, and indeed a refined revision of the cosmic holopathy proposed by Roman Stoicism. The One, for Shelley, is best figured, as in his poem by the same name, as an idealized "sensitive plant."

For Shelley, a "person" (whatever that is) achieves monistic rapport by sensitization, by stripping the insulation of matter, which includes the accretions of conventionalized Lockean psychological atomism, from the sheer electricity, the absolute "unweddedness" (the meaning of the Greek etymon for electricity), of the brain-soul dialectic. Among the aestheticized elect, this stripping or enucleating of the noumenal (archetypal) self always issues not in the triumph of time and its minions but in the apotheosis of the soul by way of Sentimental Naturalism:

Teach me half the gladness
    That thy brain must know,
Such harmonious madness
    (To a Skylark 101–3)

(George Meredith picks up on the brain-soul dialectic in lines
112-13 of the "Lark Ascending":

In the brain's reflex of yon bird:
Wherefore their soul in me, or mine).

For Shelley, the soul is ecstasy, a monadic spasm of the brain. Nature
(like Eostre's transformed bunny thinking, it is still a bird) lays an
Easter egg and hatches it, so to speak. Resurrection is merely release
from the grip of matter and its gauche restraints, into "liberty." (The
affinities between such liberty and Nietzsche's Liber, or Bacchus, or
Dionysus, are obvious.)

In what follows, the explication of several key words and phrases
will reveal that Hopkins was replying to Shelley's "To a Skylark" in
his own poem "The Caged Skylark." These are the relevant citations
from Shelley's poem:

Higher still and higher
    From the earth thou springest
Like a cloud of fire; (6–8)

Like an unbodied joy whose race is just begun. (15)

From rainbow clouds there flow not
    Drops so bright to see
As from thy presence showers a rain of melody. (33–35)

. . . thou scorner of the ground! (100)

In "To a Skylark," "ground" fades away to Ground, the ultimate Soul.
When Shelley is read in this light and perceived to be a nympholept
extraordinaire, one can understand why Paul Elmer More called him
"almost inhuman."

—Nathan Cervo, "Hopkins's *The Caged Skylark* and Shelley's *To a
Skylark*," *The Explicator* 47, no. 1 (Fall 1988): pp. 17–18.

HAROLD BLOOM ON SHELLEY'S FAREWELL TO THE INVISIBLE POWERS OF NATURE IN "TO A SKYLARK"

[Harold Bloom has written extensively on all of the Romantic poets. In the excerpt below from the chapter on Percy Bysshe Shelley in *The Visionary Company* (1961), Bloom discusses "To a Skylark" as Shelley's farewell to the theme of the invisible powers of nature and the poet.]

The beautiful ode *To a Skylark,* composed a year later, can be taken as Shelley's lyrical farewell to the theme of the power hidden behind nature and the poet's relation to that power. As the poem begins, the bird is already out of sight; it is flying too high for visibility. The poet hears the lark's song coming out of the clear, still, blue sky; the impression is astonishingly disembodied. Delighted surprise is the tone of this ecstatic first stanza:

> Hail to thee, blithe Spirit!
> Bird thou never wert,
> That from Heaven, or near it,
> Pourest thy full heart
> In profuse strains of unpremeditated art.

The unseen bird is all swiftness and fire in the second stanza; he goes on soaring and singing, higher and higher, into the blue of his happiness. He goes on until he is stopped, and he never is stopped. He moves in an upper paradise, in which infinite desire is gratified, and this is possible because, appearance aiding fancy here, he is "unbodied," he is only song.

In Stanzas IV and V, the lark is compared to the morning star, Shelley's prime emblem of desire, poetry, relationship. The lark is unseen as the star is unseen in daylight, but the clear, piercing song of the lark can be heard, as *keen* to hear as the lines of light are *keen* (that is, clear and bright) to be viewed, when the star's lamp narrows. Neither the lark's song nor the star's light fades out in dimness; rather, they vanish by intensification, until only one clear note or one clear arrow of light is left. They intensify until one hardly hears or sees them anymore, but, rather, feels that they are there.

Stanzas VI and VII continue the simile between song and light, quite straightforwardly, and the same simile flows over into Stanza

VIII, where the poet's song emanates from the light of his thought, so that this similitude has been brought over to an identity that is at the heart of the poem's meaning. The poem's central image is of an abundance of joy and song so great that it must *overflow* and graciously give itself in this effusiveness. But its nature remains hidden; Shelley's poem holds to the myth of confrontation, contenting itself with inverse analogies:

> What thou art we know not;
> What is most like thee?

Those two lines are central as we proceed to that famous series of "likes": A poet, a high-born maiden, a glow-worm golden, a rose embowered. Impatient readers may protest that they cannot see in what way a lark is like any of that series; the answer is that Shelley is not comparing the lark to them or even them to the lark, but, rather, he is comparing a series of visionary tableaux to the showering forth, the flowing over, of the lark's song. The unbidden poet singing away, obscured by the light of his own conceptions, is able to temper the world with his song. The high-born maiden, love-lorn in her tower, soothes her soul with music, and the music "overflows her bower," imparts something to others as well. The glow-worm golden (and this is an urbane jest) is screened from the view by flowers and grass, but its own appearance, "its aëreal hue," overflows, as it were, and is scattered as light among flowers and grass (the song-light simile is implied here again; the glow-worm scatters light as lark, poet, maiden scatter song). The rose, robbed by the winds, flows its musk over into those winds. In each tableau the giver of song, light, perfume is *hidden*, just as the lark is hidden; in each case also there is a giving to excess, and without the necessity of the receivers having deserved the gift. ⟨. . .⟩

The lark loves, without "love's sad satiety." The burden of mortality (Stanza XVII) is therefore not existent; "things more true and deep" about death than anything we can visualize are in the lark's possession. The inference is not that the lark knows the truth of immortality (hence its happy song) but simply that one way or the other the bird's knowledge is definite, and that, again either way, it accepts that knowledge as final.

The poem climaxes in humility:

We look before and after,
  And pine for what is not:
Our sincerest laughter
  With some pain is fraught;
Our sweetest songs are those that tell of saddest thought.

Yet if we could scorn
  Hate, and pride, and fear;
If we were things born
  Not to shed a tear,
I know not how thy joy we ever should come near.

Better than all measures
  Of delightful sound,
Better than all treasures
  That in books are found,
Thy skill to poet were, thou scorner of the ground!

Teach me half the gladness
  That thy brain must know,
Such harmonious madness
  From my lips would flow,
The world should listen then, as I am listening now.

In his prayer to be the west wind's lyre, Shelley had promised that the tumult of the wind's harmonies would take from him a deep autumnal tone, "sweet though in sadness," the paradox expressed here again in "our sweetest songs are those that tell of saddest thought." This poem ends in sadness because it has not accounted for the joy that gives life to the skylark's song. Nor has it been able to suggest what determines the bounteousness of that effluence of melody. Enough that it affirms the limitless possibility of relationship; content to be a lyric, it does not attempt finalities.

—Harold Bloom, *The Visionary Company: A Reading of English Romantic Poetry* (Ithaca: Cornell University Press, 1961): pp. 302–5.

Thematic Analysis of
"Ode to the West Wind"

"Ode to the West Wind" was begun in October 1819 and published in the *Prometheus Unbound* volume in 1820. Shelley's note to the poem tells us it was written in the Cascine wood near Florence "on a day when that tempestuous wind, whose temperature is at once mild and animating, was collecting the vapours which pour down the autumnal rains," a place where the rustling leaves are remarkably loud. In this poem, as in so much of Romantic poetry, the wind and the surrounding natural environment are thought of as linked to the poet's inner being, and thus the wind becomes a source of spiritual and poetic vitality. Shelley's "Ode to the West Wind" is an address to a powerful though invisible agent, and a wish for the blessing of poetic inspiration.

The wind can have regenerative powers, but it can also mean intimation, something stated in an indirect or concealed manner; in this sense the wind can be a messenger or prophet of things to come. Shelley will employ all of these attributes of the wind within his poem.

The structure is equally important in understanding the poem. In its most simple terms, the genre of this poem is an ode, a poem that originated in the ancient Greek world and was intended to be sung or chanted. The ode is a very formal, complexly organized poem that was meant for important state functions and ceremonies, such as a ruler's birthday, an accession, a funeral, or the unveiling of a public work. In other words, it is a mode of public address. Two types of odes can be identified in "Ode to the West Wind."

The first type is based on the odes written by Pindar (between 522 and 442 B.C.) that were designed for choric song and dance to be performed in a Dionysiac theatre (or in the Agora to celebrate athletic victories). These odes commemorated some of the highest human achievements. The tone was emotional, exalted, and intense, incorporating whatever divine myths were appropriate to the occasion. The formal structure of the Pindaric ode included an announcement of victory, praise for the champion, an invocation to the gods, and praise of the athlete's city and family. However, also incorporated within this celebratory poem were reminders of the victor's mortality, a prayer to ward off bad luck, an awareness of the pitfalls of vanity or the dangers of provoking envy in the gods, and the importance of inherent excellence. Finally, Pindar's odes were written in regular stanzas: a strophe, an antistrophe, and an epode. The strophe is the initial component the Greek chorus chanted while moving from one side of the stage to another, followed by a metrically-identical antistrophe that was chanted in accompaniment to a reverse movement and lead finally to the epode, which the chorus sung while standing still.

The second type of classical ode is named for the Latin poet Horace (65–8 B.C.), who derived his stanzaic structure from such Greek poets as Sappho. In contrast to the odes of Pindar, the Horation ode is personal rather than public, general rather than occasional, tranquil rather than intense, and contemplative and philosophic in character, intended for a private reader rather than a theatrical spectator; all of these features are found in "Ode to the West Wind."

In the English tradition, however, the ode becomes irregular, based on a structure of turn, counter-turn, and stand, a series of balanced opposites. The genre attained popularity in the 17th century with Abraham Cowley's *Pindarique Odes* in 1656, in which Cowley attempted to capture the spirit and tone of Pindar rather than a formal imitation of the classical poet. In the 18th century, the great formal odes began with John Dryden's "Ode for St. Cecilia's Day." The ode became the vehicle for expressing the sublime, lofty thoughts of intellectual and spiritual concerns.

"Ode to the West Wind" combines many of the classical elements. The first three stanzas describe the wind's changing movements in nature, while at the same time the lines vacillate between the external world and the world of the imagination. Shelley's most interesting departure from classical models is that the person being celebrated is ultimately the poet himself.

In the first lines of Section One, Shelley creates a duality for the wind; it is a spiritual agent who will take on human attributes. This accounts for its active participation in the physical world. This duality is established in the first line where the wind, like all living beings of the natural world, is a breathing entity. (In fact, the original meaning of "wind" is breath.) "O wild West Wind, thou breath of Autumn's being." In the second and third lines, however, we are immediately reminded that the West Wind comes as a spiritual messenger that performs its offices swiftly and invisibly: "Thou, from whose unseen presence the leaves dead / Are driven, like ghosts from an enchanter fleeing." Finally, the wind is also an animating source so powerful that even the dead are instilled with a quasi-liveliness that continues and intensifies throughout this first section. First, the multicolored leaves are infused with a vibrancy uncharacteristic of our notion of pale ghosts: "[y]ellow, and black, and pale, and hectic red, / Pestilence-stricken multitudes." Indeed, though we are told the leaves are dead from disease, they now assume an active afterlife, buffeted by the West Wind "[w]ho chariotest to their dark wintry bed." Even more dramatically, the leaves take on a mythic function, reminding us of ancient beliefs in the dying and reviving gods of classical mythology: "[t]he winged seeds" lying in their graves, waiting for the "azure sister of the Spring" to bring them back to life. "Wild Spirit, which art moving everywhere; / Destroyer and Preserver; hear, O hear!"

Section Two is a cloudscape, containing a scientifically detailed description of the sky and the effects of the wind as it moves through another medium. Here, Shelley is observing the clouds from his perspective along the banks of the Arno River, and he incorporates that observation for his own poetic ends. As Desmond King-Hele points out in *Shelley: His Thought and Work*, Shelley describes two types of clouds. The first is the cirrus cloud (the Latin word for curl) that appears white, streaky, and wispy, "the locks of the approaching storm." The second type of cloud is fractured, lying low in the west; it looks jagged and detached, gray and watery ("loose clouds like Earth's decaying leaves"). These clouds perform the function of messengers, "[a]ngels of rain and lightning," who bring some divine message to the poet.

Consistent with the classical elements discussed above, the clouds in Shelley's ode become actors participating in the rites sacred to Dionysus, the twice-born god of Greek mythology, born prematurely by his dying mother Semele and then carried to full term in the thigh of his father Zeus. Dionysus is perceived as both man and animal, male and female, and young and old. He is often depicted as wearing wings, considered to be immortal, powerful, and self-revelatory, the premier god of wine and intoxication. His cults are intense and violent, revolts against the established social order. Furthermore, his domain extends to the world of madness and ecstasy, theater and impersonation, as well as to the mysterious realm of the dead and the expectation of an afterlife blessed with Dionysian exultation. The common denominator that connects all these different worlds over which Dionysus presides is his ability to transcend the mortal boundaries of the physical world.

No wonder the Dionysian cult was particularly appealing to the radical Shelley. Thus, when Shelley describes the clouds, "[l]ike the bright hair uplifted from the head / Of some fierce Maenad . . . / Thou Dirge / Of the dying year," he is referring to the "maenads," female participants in the Dionysiac cult who would leave the city, crying out to the mountains, where they would let down their hair and beginning a frenzied dance to the sounds of high-pitched music.

Section Three is about the sea's response to the wind and begins with a summoning of the West Wind from "his summer dream," having been seduced by the warm Mediterranean, "[l]ulled by the coil of his chrystalline streams / Beside a pumice isle in Baiæ's bay." From this vantage point of the area surrounding the Bay, Shelley could see the ruins of imposing villas, '[a]ll overgrown with azure moss and flowers," once owned by ancient Roman emperors. "And saw in sleep old palaces and towers / Quivering within the wave's intenser day." According to the *Oxford Classical Dictionary*, Baiæ "flourished as a volcanic spa and resort, thanks to hot springs." But amidst this serenity, a great upheaval is taking place; the placid appearance of the surface waters conceals the turbulence beneath wrought by the West Wind: "While far below / The sea-blooms and the oozy woods . . . of the ocean, know / thy voice, and suddenly grow grey with fear / And tremble."

This third section ends with the same words as the two preceding sections; Shelley is addressing the West Wind for the third time: "O hear!"

Section Four of the poem begins with a recapitulation of the previous three elemental effects of the West Wind, on land, in the sky, and upon the ocean, with the important distinction that the poet now insinuates himself into the tempestuous performance of the West Wind, thereby imposing himself as the true subject of his poem. "If I were a dead leaf thou mightest bear; / If I were a swift cloud to fly with thee; / A wave to pant beneath thy power, and share / the impulse of thy strength." Furthermore, implicit within this gesture is the impetus that gave rise to the poem—the wish to be joined with the West Wind, "[t]he comrade of thy wanderings over Heaven, / . . . to outstrip thy skiey speed," to have new life infused into his imaginative powers. That wish is an invocation to the divine power of the wind, a supplication by a devoted subject burdened by mortal concerns, suffering from a diminution in his creative abilities: "[a]s thus with thee in prayer in my sore need. / Oh! Lift me as a wave, a leaf, a cloud!"

In Section Five the wish for a regenerated imagination intensifies as it becomes a plea for an inspiration akin to the Dionysiac frenzy of ancient times. "Make my thy lyre, even as the forest is / . . . Be thou, Spirit fierce, / My spirit! Be thou me, impetuous one!" It is a wish for nothing less than a complete possession by the strength of the Wind, a possession equal to the rapturous dancing of the maenads. "Drive my dead thoughts over the universe . . . And, by the incantation of this verse, / Scatter, as from an unextinguished hearth, / Ashes and sparks, my words among mankind!"

The Eolian lyre was a favorite household furnishing and an important symbol of poetic inspiration for the Romantic poets, and it is central to Coleridge's poem, "The Aeolian Harp." Named for the god Aeolus, god of the winds, and often considered to voice nature's own music, the harp (or lyre) has strings stretched across a rectangular box that respond to the passing wind with rising and falling musical chords. Similarly, the poet in "Ode to the West Wind" is identifying with the Aeolian lyre, praying that it will help spread his poetic voice throughout the land, proclaiming the message of a new beginning. The irony is that Shelley, however, cannot transcend the physical world, and so he must remain in place, hoping that the West Wind will "speak" for him. He can only wait in anxious anticipation that the wind will respond to his desperate plea: "O Wind, / If winter comes, can Spring be far behind?" ❀

Critical Views on
"Ode to the West Wind"

[François Jost is the author of *Introduction to Comparative Literature* (1974) and an editor of *Aesthetics and the Literature of Ideas: Essays in Honor of Owen Aldridge* (1990). In the excerpt below from his article, "Anatomy of an Ode: Shelley and the Sonnet Tradition," Jost discusses the complex genre of "Ode to the West Wind," and its substantial roots in classical tradition of ancient Greece and Rome.]

Each of the five stanzas of the "Ode" is divided into four tercets and a couplet. The rhyme scheme is that of the *Divina commedia*, except that Dante did not use a distich to end his cantos. He understood that one verse was sufficient for echoing the middle rhyme left in suspense in the last tercet: thus he created and practiced the classical terza rima *aba bcb cdc . . . yzy z.* The fourteenth line of his stanzas seems to be Shelley's rabbit in the hat: with a sleight of hand he transforms four terza rima tercets into a sonnet, pulling from his sleeve a Shakespearean couplet instead of a Dantesque end-line and thus metamorphosing five terza rima poems into a kind of coronet. Obviously, we will need to show that terza rima is a valid rhyme arrangement for the sonnet and that Shelley, by using it, is a poet familiar with the fundamentals of the genre, rather than a prestidigitator amazing his spectators. One critic has stated that each of the five terza rima strophes shows "the strength and compactness of a sonnet," while another one asserts that "Shelley's use of terza rima accounts in large part for the fact that none of the five stanzas of the Ode reads like a sonnet."

We must also ask the question, What more do we know about a poem by putting its title under a new rubric, that is, by saying or proving that the "Ode to the West Wind" is not only an ode but also a short sonnet cycle? The answer is that the acknowledgment and recognition of the genre or genres to which a literary work belongs may modify the reader's understanding and interpretation. The identification of the categories in which a masterpiece may be placed determines, to some degree, the mood in which the audience listens or should listen. While a classification cannot modify intrinsic values, it may reveal some concealed artistic qualities, lead to deeper insight, and thus grant a fuller enjoyment of the work. Horace's "*utile*" blends better with his "*dulce*" when a text is read in unison with its creator. Therefore the question arises: was Shelley aware, while calling his poem an ode, that he was at the same time experimenting in another genre? Or may his case be summarized by a slightly altered quotation from Austin Dobson's "Rose-Leaves": "I intended an Ode / And it turned to five Sonnets"? In fact, Shelley did write an ode, but he knew better than some of his critics that a poem may at one and the same time belong to several literary species. He was conscious not only of the aesthetic but also of the technical characteristics of his poem. One of the most striking of those technical characteristics is the reduction of generic ambiguity into poetic unity.

Shelley's thoughts are deeply rooted in antiquity. To understand the complexities of his genius, his readers must be classicists. Already some of his earliest works reveal his fascination for Aeschylus' and Homer's Greece; he translated a few *Dialogues* of Plato, and his last drama was *Hellas* (1821). Poetical, sentimental, and political motivations joined in developing, from André Chénier to Novalis and Byron, the philhellenism that marked some of the most distinguished pre-Romantics and Romantics all over Europe. In 1772 the twenty-three-year-old Goethe wrote to Herder: "Ich wohne jetzt in Pindar." One year later his drama *Götz von Berlichingen* appeared, announcing "Sturm und Drang." How does one reconcile the two trends? The study of romanticism must include a chapter on the "classicisme des romantiques." Shelley not only adopted ancient forms into which he would pour modern substance, he also revised and renewed them. Out of five sonnets—if we may once more beg the question—he made a poem which belongs to a venerable tradition, the ode. The theme of the "Ode" and also the key in which it is composed—with some reservations concerning the last two stanzas—fit perfectly with the genre he chose.

Another question: is Shelley's "Ode" in the Pindaric or the Horatian tradition? At first glance it reveals all the major traits of the Roman type. Its linear sequence of structurally identical stanzas leads to the triumphal hope: "If Winter comes, can Spring be far behind?" The "Ode," however, offers characteristics of the Greek type as well. The first three stanzas together constitute the Pindaric strophe: the leaf, the cloud, and the wave join in shaping the central idea: the earthly, "a-theological" notion of the infinite does not come from scholastic philosophy. The leaf, the cloud, and the wave symbolize the transient: the leaf, which belongs to the earth; the cloud, which is air; and the water of the sea. The three inseparable elements mingle in the first three sonnets. The fourth element, however, although mentioned in passing at the end of the second stanza, finds its function only in the remaining two. The wind will scatter Shelley's fiery word "as from an unextinguished hearth / Ashes and sparks." The fire Shelley refers to is not to be found in the physical world but in the creator's, in the poet's soul. Thus the "Ode" is thematically divided into two contrasting parts. In the second, the reader may recognize a kind of epode rather than an antistrophe. The Pindaric ode, triadic in essence, has been truncated.

Still other considerations may be significant. In Shelley's bipartite poem, the opposition between the first three stanzas and the last two conforms to the basic principles underlying the structure of the sonnet. In the second part of the "Ode," Shelley endows the anonymous third-person singer of the first part with a personality, his own: "If I were a dead leaf thou mightest bear." Such a sharp contrast is characteristic of the sonnet, not of the classical ode in which the author remains invisible or has only a marginal, rhetorical function. No ancient poet would ever think of an "Ode to myself." Nothing like "My heart aches" or "If I were a dead leaf" can be found, either in Pindar or in Horace, though their carmina—called "odes" only by later commentators—do not always treat the dignified topics one might expect. Such sighs and dreams belong to Keats and Shelley and to their generation. For critics who choose to ignore the historical evolution of literary species, neither the "West Wind" nor the "Nightingale" is an ode. By the same token, however, these critics must argue that the stanzas in question are not sonnets.

—François Jost, "Anatomy of an Ode: Shelley and the Sonnet Tradition," *Comparative Literature* 34, no. 3 (Summer 1982): pp. 224–26.

[Jennifer Wagner is the author of *A Moment's Monument: Revisionary Poetics and the Nineteenth-Century English Sonnet* (1996). In the excerpt below from her article, "A Figure of Resistance: The Visionary Reader in Shelley's Sonnets and the 'West Wind' *Ode*," Wagner discusses the poem's deliberate "openendedness" which creates the possibility of interpretive change and development, and a "place" that acknowledges the importance of the reader within that evolutionary process of interpretation.]

Percy Bysshe Shelley is not a "sonneteer"; he never wrote sonnets systematically, as did many of his contemporaries—Wordsworth and Coleridge, Keats and Hunt—and we have no critical comments on the form from him. And yet he is an eminent sonnet-writer, the few sonnets he did write displaying a mastery and comprehension of the form and its power. To no small degree, these poems are indebted to Wordsworth's sonnets for that power, partaking of an authority—in the most complex sense of that word—that emerged from Wordsworth's own revision of the Miltonic sonnet. ⟨...⟩

Shelley's sonnets were sparked by the same large ambition, by that same Miltonic fire, but to describe them as Wordsworthian in mode is to risk diminishing their originality. While Shelley keenly recognizes the inspiration underlying Wordsworth's authorial sonnet voice, he does not accept that authority uncritically. Indeed this poet's critique of Wordsworth's monolithic stance is matched by a pressuring of the form itself. The construction of Shelley's sonnets suggests that the poet recognized *closure* as form's most tyrannical element, closing off the poem from any possibility of change or development—for these sonnets are characterized by an openendedness that resists an ending. The implications of that are hardly incidental. The openendedness of the sonnet space, which Wordsworth so clearly associated with "mental space," leads toward a revised view of subjectivity that better serves Shelley's revolutionary politics. In *The Poetry of Life: Shelley and Literary Form*, Ronald Tetreault argues that Shelley's notion of authorial subjectivity is "decentred" in his public poems by his awareness of *the reader*. This participation of the reader "generates a process by which meanings come to be shared, but this process is a dialogical one in which the 'otherness' of readers' intentions is acknowledged."

That acknowledgment of the reader in that "mental space" certainly informs the sonnets, and underlies an effort to destabilize the authority of the speaker in favor of the reader. The poems' openendedness is a refusal to monumentalize a single vision—as that results only in the kind of tyrannical habits of thinking that Shelley loathes—by deferring finally to the interpretation of the reader himself. The sonnet remains the radiant figure that Wordsworth envisions it, its tropological momentum directed outward—but its agency is directed now toward the future, not toward the conflation of past and present that we see in Wordsworth's visionary sonnets. Shelley's notion of the temporality of the sonnet tends toward the apocalyptic, but it is essentially anticipatory, rather than retrospective.

Shelley's significant early poems include "Sonnet: To a Balloon Laden with Knowledge" and "Sonnet: On Launching Some Bottles Filled with Knowledge into the Bristol Channel," both composed in August 1812. In both poems, "knowledge" is figured as a radiance that, when the balloon itself is burst or the bottle opened, will project itself beyond those vessels to become, in the first sonnet, "A watch-light," "A beacon in the darkness of the Earth," "A Sun which, o'er the renovated scene, / Shall dart like Truth where Falsehood yet has been." In the second sonnet ("On launching some Bottles...") knowledge is a radiance that will gleam "from pole to pole, / And tyrant-hearts with powerless envy burst / To see their night of ignorance dispersed." If we may for a moment take these images of vessels as images of poetic form as well, what Shelley is trying to imagine is a way in which the contents are liberated from the form itself. Form is troped not simply as containment, but as an active "vehicle" of the dispersement of power—and thus as somehow "open-ended."

These crucial early sonnets already suggest a role for poetic form in Shelley's revolutionary and apocalyptic vision of the world, about which so much has already been written. ⟨. . .⟩ That recognition is accompanied, however, by a sense of irony, disappointed as Shelley was by what he saw as Wordsworth's political apostasy and as a misuse of his imagination's visionary power.

—Jennifer Wagner, "A Figure of Resistance: The Visionary Reader in Shelley's Sonnets and the 'West Wind' Ode," *Southwest Review* 77, no. 1 (Winter 1992): pp. 109–11.

[Edward Duffy is the author of *Rousseau in England: The Context for Shelley's Critique of the Enlightenment* (1979). In the excerpt below from his article, "Where Shelley Wrote and What He Wrote For," Duffy discusses "Ode to the West Wind" in terms of its historical context: the disappointed hopes of a post-Napoleonic Europe (1819). The poem's speaker offers himself as the exemplary victim who will bring forth a much-needed "spiritual redemption."]

The natural force invoked by the ode is explicitly "wild," and many critics have suggested that the poem itself could have been less unharnessed, more focused in theme, and more disciplined in choice of word and image. To dispose of the first objection about theme, it is only necessary to recall that in post-Napoleonic 1819, the spirit of the age was, to one of Shelley's experience and opinions, the spirit of destruction and disappointed hopes. This "breath of Autumn's being" was so enthralling to Shelley because, as drawn into the semantic cluster of wind, breath, and spirit, it struck him as a patent signifier for what lay destructively behind the winter of his own and Europe's discontent. The overall strategy of the poem conforms closely to Kenneth Burke's theory that, typically, a literary form is a strategic renaming of a situation. The poem begins with a natural model for the deplorably chained and bowed state of post-Napoleonic Europe, and then it contrives to rename this theater of repression and disappointment as but a necessary prelude to renewal—the preserver acting, for the time being, as destroyer. The speaker of the ode steps forward and becomes an exemplary victim of his times. Surrendering himself to a wind that he himself has inflected into a "spirit," he writes from a Golgotha of passion that is conscious of its many predecessors: a Christ crowned with thorns; a diseased Job in verbal contest with his God; a soon-to-be-crippled Jacob wrestling with the angel until that angel bless him. The ambition of Shelley's ode is the ambition of those Hebrew prophets whose Old Testament culmination is the suffering servant of Second Isaiah, a suffering servant "chosen," proclaims Isaiah, but "chosen in the furnace of affliction." Like his Old Testament precursor, Shelley offers himself as an exemplary victim of his community's failings, the faults of that community whipped into his flesh so graphically that its culpable moral state must become undeniably clear and a turnaround from that culpability the one pressing item on the moral and spiritual agenda.

The ode's final appeal that the wind scatter its words among mankind is the thoroughly practical appeal of a serious writer. Behind it, there lies a simple fact of Shelley's career: a published writer for more than a decade, this would-be herald of the millennium still lacked an audience, his "leaves" falling dead off the printing press and bound for nothing but oblivion. And so, with the beginning of the ode's fourth stanza, all the inanimate multitudes in thrall to the west wind abruptly precipitate into the one sharply defined picture of a hitherto ineffectual writer and reformer, who by surrendering to the power of the wind would now hope to write of his and his community's failures with the vividness of stigmata, with an authority no more to be withstood than the breath of the fierce wind itself. What Shelley wants from the wind is authority, the poet-prophet praying that the raw power of the wind, the raw power of the way things are, might batter him into the oracular peremptoriness of one whose fellows must listen to him because, in this other's fate, they cannot help but see their collective own. At first chained and bowed like Prometheus, the speaker will finally come to embrace the lashing rod of actuality because he will finally come to re-see it, to re-name it, as the magic wand conducting the "incantation of this verse," the scepter of power that has already rid him of his adolescent delusions "when to outstrip thy skiey speed scarce seemed a vision," is now driving that vision into Atlantic depths of fear and trembling, and might yet confer on "his words among mankind" the authority of one who has suffered what he writes. In "Ode to the West Wind," a self-consciously failed writer turns his failure into the sign that his words are in season for a time of endemic failure, and into the hope that these words might yet be the trumpet of a prophecy to an earth so unawakened that it knows not what it is doing or what it is having done to it. ⟨. . .⟩

In "Ode to the West Wind," the wind is a God-figure narrowed into the political, social and cultural sphere. It is what devastatingly is in post-Napoleonic Europe. Before this "breath of Autumn's being" the entire canvas of Italy blackens toward a Golgotha of winter. By poem's end, however, this same breath has become the no less divine impetus for a regenerative push toward oracle. What effects this turnaround is not the inevitable and merely physical cycle of the seasons, but the speaking human figure at the center of the poem, in and as he is driven toward a dramatic climax of self-recognition, a self-recognition the exact wording of which drives him and his reader all the way back to one of the most privileged texts of our civilization. For the speaker's self-recognition as one who has "striven with thee in prayer in my sore need" builds upon that chapter in *Genesis* where Jacob, the father of the twelve tribes, wrestles with the angel of Yahweh, is crippled by him, but will not let him go until, in blessing him, he rename him Israel—(in Hebrew) "he who strives with God" (*Genesis* 32:22–31).

—Edward Duffy, "Where Shelley Wrote and What He Wrote For: The Example of 'The Ode to the West Wind,'" *Studies in Romanticism* 23, no. 3 (Fall 1984): pp. 360–63.

SIMON HAINES ON THE WIND AS BREATH AND SPIRIT

[In the excerpt below from his 1997 book *Shelley's Poetry*, Simon Haines gives a structural analysis of the "Ode to the West Wind," indicating several interpretive tensions in both its form and content, specifically relating to the wind as breath or spirit.]

The "Ode to the West Wind" is in five stanzas, each one a kind of sonnet, a fourteen-line structure in iambic pentameter containing four *terza rima* verses with a concluding couplet. The five stanzas together comprise a seventy-line address to and invocation of the "wild West Wind," also called "Wild Spirit," referred to repeatedly as "thou." The first three stanzas enumerate the qualities of the Wind itself, while the last two, as foreshadowed by the ritualistic phrase "O hear!" at the end of each of the first three, concern themselves principally with the speaker or invoker and with his relation to the Wind. Thus there is a "turn" in the poem's focus three-fifths of the way through, from the hearer of the invocation to what that hearer is going to be asked to hear, roughly corresponding to the usual "turn" in a sonnet after eight of its fourteen lines. The sonnet form is thereby reduplicated on a larger scale. Broadly speaking, it is the treatment of the Wind's qualities in the first three stanzas which has given rise to most of the explicit disagreement about the poem, but it is the treatment in the last two of the invoker which must chiefly determine one's response to the attitude of the poem as a whole.

In the first three stanzas (readers will need the text before them) the poetry seems to concern itself less with a relationship than with a kind of entity. That entity is not so much what Wilson Knight called a "true object" which is "in some mysterious way more us than itself" as an unseen power or presence external to us, a something which blows, drives, chariots, moves, destroys and preserves the visible things of the world whilst remaining invisible itself. It is not so much a Bloomean "thou" which is also an "I" as an object of the speaker's perception which is nevertheless more than an "It." We are not so much in a "world in which Nature wears a human face" as in a natural world of leaves, seeds, buds, clouds, waves and sea-blooms, all driven by an inhuman power. This entity, power or presence is a version of the Shelleyan Power we have become familiar with, the one he spent his life as a poet trying to represent in either its transcendent or its immanent aspect, the one whose "awful shadow . . . Floats though unseen amongst us" in the "Hymn to Intellectual Beauty," the one called Necessity in *Queen Mab* and *Alastor*, the one whose secret strength informed the universe of things in "Mont Blanc." There is reason to believe that Shelley himself thought the "Ode" to have been one of his most successful representations and discoveries of this Power. At the end of his notebook draft of the poem appears, in an excited scribble, a quotation in Greek from Euripides' *Hercules Furens*. The quotation translated reads: "By virtue I, a mortal, defeat you, a great god." In this poem the god takes the form of the West Wind, and is perceptible primarily to hearing and touch, although its "shape" is discernible when visible things are attached to or driven by it, as a magnetic field can be "seen" in the movement and position of the iron filings within its influence. Clearly, however, the Wind, or the Spirit that for the moment is the Wind, is more than just an unseen physical presence; this is more than a description of a travelling thunderstorm. There is a crucial determining figure of thought beneath the surface of the poem: that just as the existence of an entity imperceptible to some of the senses may be induced from the evidence of the other senses, so the existence of an entity imperceptible to all the senses may be induced from the evidence of the senses alone. Claims that Shelley's imagination is directly in contact with an ideal object notwithstanding, he is using the sensory world as the enabling material of his thought, and imagining the object of his thought as an experiential object: as an idea, perhaps, but one held in a quasi-sensory way. Moreover, he is using ordinary language as the enabling medium of his thought, and ordinary language has its own resistance and momentum. ⟨...⟩

In its first line, for example, the Wind is addressed as "thou breath of Autumn's being." In the first place if Shelley means by this that the Wind is the breath of the being of Autumn, and not that it is the being of the breath of Autumn (both are syntactically possible), why even so does he wish to address the Wind in this way, and not simply as "thou breath of Autumn"? If we are to take the poem as seriously as Shelley apparently wished us to take it, and took it himself, we must assume that there is an important difference between "Autumn" and "Autumn's being."

—Simon Haines, *Shelley's Poetry: The Divided Self* (New York: St. Martin's Press, 1997): pp. 152–54.

G. K. BLANK ON THE TRANSFORMATION OF POETIC ANXIETY

[G. K. Blank is the author of *Wordsworth's Influence on Shelley: A Study of Poetic Authority* (1988) and *Wordsworth and Feeling: The Poetry of an Adult Child* (1995). In the excerpt below from the article, "Shelley's Wind of Influence," Blank discusses Shelley's transforming the "anxiety of influence" of his poetic forbears into a "transitory moment" preceding his own poem.]

Contemporary influence is unavoidable and necessary for creating superior art, notes Shelley, adding that man is a creature highly susceptible to being modified and influenced: he is impressionable, hyper-sensitive, and predisposed to affectability. Shelley holds that influence is as inevitable as it is pervasive, yet even so the poet must be sensitive to it, using it with sensitivity. A poet both mirrors and modifies all of what influences him, and he can, if he is a superior poet, add his own influence to the greater force. In this way he will, in a relative manner, achieve originality, thus becoming both a creator and creation of his age. Shelley's remarkable feat of reasoning is that he comes to both acknowledge his anxiety over the problem of influence and to use it as a source of creative strength. For Shelley, inspiration is that transitory moment of exchange preceding the creative act when the force of influence and the poet touch each other. But the problem is not just how to find inspiration, but how to maintain or retain its fleeting and fading powers, how to translate it into that formal creative mode known as poetry.

What I wish to pursue in this essay is a reading of the *Ode to the West Wind* (1820) as a poetic expression of the need to be a poet, as Shelley's most important and agonizing allegory of his desire to be influenced and influential. The speaker of the poem attempts to "locate" his place in a scene where he hopes to engage the force of influence in that moment of inspiration. And accompanying his invocations for lifting and scattering, for bleeding and blowing, for becoming a leaf, cloud, or wave, he demands that the wind make him a prophetic poet. The *Ode* thus poetically enacts Shelley's ultimate desire to be the legislating poet. This essay examines the ways that the speaker creates himself as a poet, and the strategies by which the poet displaces the West Wind as the central figure in the poem. ⟨. . .⟩

The critical history of the *Ode to the West Wind* shows the typical range of response we have come to expect from Shelley's interpreters. On one hand, after examining some lines of the *Ode*, Leavis concluded that Shelley's poetry exhibits a "weak grasp on the actual." On the other hand, investigators have gone to great lengths to demonstrate that Shelley's poem is soundly based on geographical and meteorological facts. Indeed, in 1972 a photograph and a detailed diagram of the west wind's movement as Shelley would have observed it at the particular place and time of year appeared on the pages of *The Times Literary Supplement*. Shelley himself may have started the trouble when he included a footnote to his poem explaining where he wrote the poem and what the weather was like. But often a fallacy of interpretation occurs in such a note: it is mistaken for the subject matter or idea of the poem, rather than as a poetic convention. The note merely gives placement of composition, and says nothing at all about the poem's content. ⟨. . .⟩

The structural nature of the poem is important to note because each part acts as a unit and has its own "tropological" logic and theme which combines with the whole. And as we will see, form and content antithetically interplay in the *Ode*: the highly-controlled structure is counter-balanced by the apparently uncontrollable subject of the poem. Thus we can anticipate viewing the *Ode* as the speaker's attempt to display and sustain his poetic powers.

In the first part of the poem the West Wind is described as an invisible mover and carrier. It is a pervasive force, and although we tend to think of the west wind as a revitalizing energy, this particular wind's function in this first part is, as an "unseen presence," to drive dead leaves and to bear seeds to their "dark" and "cold" graves. The West Wind is not "Autumn's being" but the "*breath* of Autumn's being." This differentiation is important because it serves to show that it is the wind/breath element that is the moving power. The obvious connection with the "unseen presence" is the "unseen Power" of Intellectual Beauty (*Hymn*) and the "unseen" Skylark (*Skylark*), both of which can also be seen to be representative of poetic inspiration. ⟨...⟩

The West Wind joins these other invisible forces, but its importance is as an energy that will give rise to further forces. It is not an end in itself, and rather more a cause than an effect. It is both preparatory (preparing the seeds for growth) and anticipatory (anticipating the "living" elements that will come). The role of the West Wind in this context is what makes it simultaneously a "Destroyer and preserver": in the process of preserving life for the future, the life of the past is cleared away. Old leaves make way for new buds. Moreover, decayed leaves become the humus in which the new life will begin.

—G. K. Blank, "Shelley's Wind of Influence," *Philological Quarterly* 64, no. 4 (Fall 1985): pp. 475–77.

Bryan Shelley on the Wind as Renewal

[Bryan Shelley is the author of "The Synthetic Imagination: Shelley and Associationism," (1983). In the excerpt below from his book, *Shelley and Scripture: The Interpreting Angel*, Shelley identifies three biblical sources for the "Ode to the West Wind," showing in each instance that the wind is associated with the concept of renewal.]

In the Scriptures, the wind heralds the new epochs of the post-diluvian world (Gen. 8: 1) and of the Church age (Acts 2: 2). Jesus compares the person who has been 'born of the Spirit' with the wind, in that both are enigmatic (John 3: 8). What links these three passages is the idea of renewal. Each could apply to the ode in a particular way. The speaker in the poem is aware of an impending new epoch; he emphasizes spiritual rebirth; and just as the coming of the Holy Spirit brought with it the gift of prophecy (Acts 2: 18), so the ode is self-conscious of a prophetic role. Whether it is seen as structurally akin to a prayer, a psalm, a hymn, or even an exorcism (based on l. 3), it is more fundamentally a prophetic lyric. The prophets were masters at employing a controlling image to illustrate a point. The central picture in Shelley's poem is that of the forest, which is analogous to the poet. It recalls the biblical simile in which the man who puts his trust in the Lord is compared to a tree planted by the water, whose leaves do not wither. The Psalmist contrasts this picture of the righteous man with that of the ungodly one, who is 'like the chaff which the wind driveth away' (Ps. 1: 4). Steadfastness is the opposite of being subject to the wind. Shelley, however, seems to combine the symbolism of tree and chaff. He likens himself to the trees, but not in the sense of having stability, for his leaves in fact wither only to be driven before the wind like chaff. Prophetically, the wind is an agent of judgement, ferreting out that which is perishable (Isa. 64: 6; Ps. 1: 4, 6). Its counterpart is the verdant image, which connotes stability and prosperity (Ps. 1: 3). In prostrating himself emotionally before the wind, the poet reverses its biblical significance, for his 'chaff' is not transitory, but conducive to rebirth.

It is quite possible that in his opening stanza, Shelley may have had in mind one of the visions of the prophet Zechariah. His 'chaff'—a frenetic mêlée of yellow, black, pale, and red leaves which are survived by the wind-borne charioted seeds—is similar to the four chariots seen by the prophet (6: 1–8). Each of these is seen drawn by a group of horses coloured differently from those with the other chariots. Respectively, they are red, black, white, and bay (mixed with 'grisled'). They are the 'four spirits of the heavens' (Zech. 6: 5) which can be linked with the 'four winds of the heaven' described earlier (2: 6). The white and black horses execute God's judgement on Israel's enemy to the north, apparently Babylon. But for failing to observe the Yahwistic ethical norms, the Israelites themselves incur chastisement; they are 'scattered . . . with a whirlwind' sent by God, leaving a verdant land to become wilderness (Zech. 7: 14). As in the imagery of the Psalmist, wind is a means of castigation; its counterpoise is the verdant landscape. Shelley's petitioning of the wind could therefore be an invocation of judgement, a correcting process that may involve revolution. The leaves of the natural world, then, are presented symbolically—at least in terms of the biblical prophecy—as elements subject to a sovereign power. In Shelley's own life, the dispersed leaves are the pages of the proselytic literature which he had issued, much like the bottles of knowledge that he had deployed at Lynmouth Beach, Devon, in 1812.

Like *Peter Bell the Third*, the ode is Job-like in some key respects. As in the biblical drama, the operations of nature are adduced as mysteries to differentiate the limitations of finite human comprehension from the unlimited capacities of an imperceptible source of power. Answering Job from the whirlwind, the voice of Yahweh declares: 'Who hath divided a watercourse for the overflowing of waters, or a way for the lightning of thunder; To cause it to rain on the earth . . . and to cause the bud of the tender herb to spring forth?' (Job 38:25-7). Shelley employs the similar imagery of buds (stanza I), rain and lightning (stanza II), and cloven waters (stanza III). Each of their associated emblems of leaf, cloud, and wave is endowed with motion by the wind. But the speaker, bound by his temporality, could only fall to the ground in an attempt to respond as they do. He feels all too keenly his human limitations, and might have lamented with Job, 'wilt thou bring me into dust again?' (Job 10: 9), or 'Thou liftest me up to the wind . . . and dissolvest my substance' (Job 30: 22). He compensates for this sense of limitation by imaging himself as the instrument which the wind will play, yielding his power of speech to the prerogative of the 'other.'

By transforming the poem into an incantation, the speaker in the ode ritually purifies his lips from the custom of merely uttering a poem, as the unclean lips of Isaiah were purified by a live coal taken from the altar by one of the seraphim (Isa. 6: 6–8). The act of purification was necessary for the prophet to become a bearer of God's message. The incantation effectively transforms the main elements of the poem—forest and leaves—into the new elements of 'unextinguished hearth' and '[a]shes and sparks.'

—Bryan Shelley, *Shelley and Scripture: The Interpreting Angel* (New York: Oxford University Press, 1994): pp. 92–94.

Thematic Analysis of
"Adonais"

Written and published on October 4, 1821, "Adonais" memorializes the death of Shelley's friend and fellow poet John Keats, whom he regarded as being one of the poets of "the highest genius" of the age. Keats died in Rome on February 23, 1821, at the age of twenty-six. A medical doctor by training, Keats knew for some time that he was seriously ill. Indeed, on the evening of February 3, 1820, he had coughed up blood and knew he had no choice but to face the inevitable. "I cannot be deceived in that colour; that drop of blood is my death warrant. I must die."

Despite the actual circumstances of Keats's demise, Shelley chose to construct an elaborate myth, based partly on Greek mythology and partly on the literary "politics" of his day, specifically blaming his friend's death on a scathing review of Keats's poem "Endymion" in the April issue of the 1818 *Quarterly Review*, written by a then anonymous critic (since identified as John Wilson Croker). Shelley is referring to this literary critic when he speaks of the devastating effect of his review on his beloved and sensitive friend as "the curse of Cain / Light on his head who pierced thy innocent breast, / And scared the angel soul that was its earthly guest!" Shelley's tirade, both within the preface, where he states that "these wretched men know not what they do," and throughout the poem, cost Shelley his already tentative relationship with *Blackwood's* magazine. But in terms of the poem, Shelley's weaving together of a contemporary situation with the primarily classical depiction of Adonis makes the work still more complex. To do this, Shelley employs two very important Greek myths in this poem.

The predominant one is the myth of Adonis (whose name also means "Lord"), in which Adonis is born from a myrrh tree, dies in a hunting accident where he is slain by a boar, and then is metamorphosed into an anemone, a flower without scent. In Shelley's poem, Adonais is killed by an evil critic, depicted as a wild beast who "pierced by the shaft which flies / In darkness" and is mourned by his mother Urania (Aphrodite/Urania, the goddess of earthly love), whom Shelley elevates to the status of motherhood, thereby invalidating another mythic tradition which has Aphrodite as Adonis's lover. Shelley did this in order to conform to the dignity of a poem written to commemorate the death of a great poet.

The second though less obvious myth concerns the story of Echo and Narcissus, which is most fully preserved by the Latin poet Ovid. In Ovid's *Metamorphoses*, Echo was a nymph who fell in love with Narcissus. Echo was punished by Hera, the wife of Zeus, for trying to distract Hera from recognizing Zeus's amorous dalliance with the other nymphs. She is punished by Hera for misusing the gift of speech for deceitful purposes and is transformed into stone; most cruelly, she can never again utter a single word or thought of her own. She is left with only the ability to echo someone else's words. In short, Echo is guilty of rhetorical violence, which bears a striking similarity to the violence wrought by the pen of Keats's reviewer. Echo also fell in love with Narcissus, a beautiful young boy who loved no one until, while gazing upon the calm surface of a lake, he fell in love with his own reflected image. This self-consuming love became deadly, for he was prohibited from ever knowing or loving another person. Though Echo would call out to him, he would never be aware of her. Narcissus was eventually metamorphosed into a beautiful white flower, an image repeated in "Adonais." The two lovers were doomed to never know each other.

Finally, "Adonais" is also a part of the classical tradition in that it is structured along the lines of the classical elegy, a type of poem inspired by the death of an important person. Although there were variations within the genre, the elegy contained certain standard structural parts:

- a ceremonial mourning for an exemplary person;
- a mournful invocation to a muse;
- a sympathetic participation of nature, who shares the mourners' grief;
- a description of the procession of appropriate mourners;
- a denunciation of unworthy participants who are found wanting in their literary achievements;
- a song of lament for the person's death;
- praise for the lost one's virtues;
- and a consolation or turning point for the poet, and for all those who share his grief, from the despair of terrible loss to hope for a far better life in heaven.

The elegy has also been used for political purposes, which is relevant to Shelley's belief that "poets are the unacknowledged legislators of their time."

Stanza 1 begins in total despair: "I weep for Adonais—he is dead!" This hopelessness will eventually be worked out in the process of the poem. Indeed, "Adonais" is what modern psychology would call "a work of mourning" in which the bereaved person goes through a catalogue of associations with the deceased and gradually accepts their absence by turning those associations into cherished memories that live on forever. Moreover, the "echoing" device, or repetition of the same phrase, "O, weep for Adonais!" that exists throughout the poem is symptomatic of the early stages of mourning.

This stanza also contains another classical device known as the "personification of the hours," in which Time is addressed as an essential living entity that marks both the passage of time and the change of seasons. Here, Time is even further particularized into the appropriate "Hour" that establishes a sympathetic rapport and becomes a trusted companion of the bereaved poet who has presided over the death of Adonais: "And thou, sad Hour, selected from all years / To mourn our loss, rouse thy obscure compeers / And teach them thine own sorrow."

In **Stanza 2** we find the classical invocation, a request for assistance, addressed to the Muses, goddesses upon whom poets depend for the inspiration needed to create their poetry. Here, that goddess is Urania, and the invocation is not only a plea for a response, but an accusation as well. The poet is angry at Urania's absence, believing that her intervention would have prevented Adonais's death. "Where wert thou might Mother, when he lay, / When thy Son lay, pierced by the shaft . . . where was lorn Urania / When Adonais died?" Shelley considers her to be negligent in her duties, ignoring her son's desperate plight. "She sate, while one, with soft enamoured breath, / Rekindled all the fading melodies, / With which, like flowers that mock the corse beneath." Indeed, Urania is vaguely implicated in the myth of Narcissus, for she too remained unresponsive to her son's echoing voice. In **Stanza 3**, Shelley must call out to her to attend to her sacred duties for she has not yet acknowledged the tragedy that has taken place. "Wake, melancholy Mother, wake and weep! / . . . For he is gone, where all things wise and fair / Descend;—oh, dream not that the amorous Deep / Will yet restore him to the vital air." She is being summoned to a terrible and unrelieved anguish. "Death feeds on his mute voice, and laughs at our despair."

Stanza 6 not only continues the implication of Urania, reminding the neglectful mother of the enormity of her loss, but expands it even further to include images of the shattered dreams and lost potential of her young son who now lives merely as a white flower on the surface of a lake. "But now, thy youngest, dearest one, has perished— / The nursling of thy widowhood, who grew, / Like a pale flower by some sad maiden cherished . . . Thy extreme hope, the loveliest and the last . . . Died on the promise of the fruit, is waste; The broken lily lies—" That lost potential for even greater artistic achievement is intensified later in **Stanza 9**, as we are given a brief catalog of the fruits of his poetic imagination, with Shelley making reference to such pastoral poems as Keats's "Ode to a Grecian Urn" and the mythological beings that are painted upon its surface. "O, weep for Adonais!—The quick Dreams, / The passion-winged Ministers of thought, Who were his flocks . . . and whom he taught / The love which was its music, wander not,—Wander no more, from kindling brain to brain, / But droop there."

In **Stanzas 14 through 17** we see Nature in sympathetic bond with Shelley's grief, for Nature recognizes that Keats loved her; the elements must respond to the terrible loss of their loving representative. "All he had loved, and moulded into thought, / From shape, and hue, and odour, and sweet sound, / Lamented Adonais . . . Pale Ocean in unquiet slumber lay, / And the wild winds flew round, sobbing in their dismay." Even Echo is resurrected in Stanza 15 from her "deathlike" state, only to a more heightened experience of her awful pain, for she can no longer even echo another person's thoughts. "Lost Echo sits amid the voiceless mountains, / . . . And will no more reply to winds or fountains, / . . . Since she can mimic not his lips, more dear / Than those for whose disdain she pined away." And so the list continues, with Keats's poems coming to life to add their plaintive voices, a truly "unspeakable" agony that finally outdoes that of Echo and Narcissus. "Grief made the young Spring wild, and she threw down / Her kindling buds, as if she Autumn were . . . since her delight is flown / . . . Nor to himself Narcissus, as to both / Thou Adonais."

In Stanza 17, the focus shifts to a denunciation of the unworthy literary practitioner, the anonymous, evil critic, who is to be forever punished for his contribution to "rhetorical violence." More significant, this is contextualized in a far more emphatic way: "As Albion wails for thee: the curse of Cain / Light on his head who pierced thy innocent breast, / And scared the angel soul that was its earthly guest." Two things are important here. First, in using the name Albion, Shelley now invokes the entire English nation, as Albion is an older name for England. Second, in comparing the reviewer to Cain, the stakes become much higher and far more realistic than any mythology; the biblical analogue also gives a sacred dimension to Keats's very being. Yet, that angelic soul has not yet been reunited with Cain's body, for it is frightened by his murderous deed. His sin lives on and holds him in captivity, and in the absence of a reunion of body with the soul, he can find no transcendental resolution to his predicament. This unrealized reunion, which would enable the deceased to break out of the shackles of his earthly bondage and live in total happiness in the next world, is especially poignant in lines reminiscent of Shelley's "Ode to the West Wind."

Stanzas 18–21 are Shelley's personal expression of grief for the loss of his friend. When he exclaims, "Ah woe is me! Winter is come and gone, / But grief returns with the revolving year," we are struck by the sense of hopeless in the last lines of Shelley's great ode. We find no spiritual renewal at this point in his elegy. Shelley is overwhelmed with abject despair, and his feelings of grief are contrasted with a regenerated natural world: "Through wood and stream and field and hill and Ocean / A quickening life from the Earth's heart has burst . . . they illumine death . . . [for] Nought we know, dies." And, finally, in **stanzas 22–29**, this mortal agony finally touches Adonais's mother Urania, causing her to accept the terrible tragedy that has taken place. At last she participates in the mourning process that until now she has evaded. "Swift as a Thought by the snake Memory stung, / From her ambrosial rest the fading Splendour sprung. / . . . so swept her on her way / Even to the mournful place where Adonais lay." This mythic being even enters into Shelley's myth of death-dealing reviewers, fiendishly depicted as "the herded wolves . . . the obscene ravens, clamorous o'er the dead; The vultures to the conqueror's banner." In denouncing them, he invokes the image of the poet Byron who wrote a satirical poem against these very same offending critics, entitled "English Bards and Scotch Reviewers" (1809). Byron's mythological analogue is Apollo, "[t]he Pythian of the age," the champion who killed the dragon Python.

In **stanzas 30–35**, Shelley turns his attention to a procession of mourners, "the mountain shepherds." In the context of "Adonais," these poetic practitioners are worthy of esteem, and preeminent among them is the poet Byron: "The Pilgrim of Eternity, whose fame / Over his living head like Heaven is bent." This is a reference to Byron's poem, "Childe Harold," concerning a young and eloquent noble of the same name who travels through a wasteland, "a place of agony and strife," like one outcast (similar to Shelley), an "outlaw of his own dark mind."

Finally, however, the unmitigated grief that has thus far dominated the poem begins to lighten. We find cause for new hope as the poet radically shifts from mourning to a denial of death's ultimate victory. The poet finds consolation for this terrible loss, and that consolation is likewise a process. In **stanza 38**, Keats becomes one of the "enduring dead," because his spirit lives on and returns, "[b]ack to the burning fountain whence it came," with the same creative powers it manifested in its mortal lifetime. The denial of death goes even further, as Shelley declares that Keats's death has been but a dream from which he now awakens. Even more boldly, he asserts that we the living are the ones who are asleep, and thus we are the ones who must strive against unknown fears and demons. "Peace, peace! He is not dead, he doth not sleep— / He hath awakened from the dream of life— / 'Tis we, who lost in stormy visions, keep / With the phantoms an unprofitable strife." Keats, having "outsoared the shadow of our night," has far surpassed and out-distanced the narrow circumference of our own lives that are filled with unrest and the fear of growing old. We are directed to stop grieving, for "[h]e lives, he wakes–'tis Death is dead, not he; / Mourn not for Adonais." Adonais no longer needs Nature's sympathy, for one of his poetic genius and sensitivity has earned his reward.

Having celebrated so poignantly Nature's eternal promise of youth and vitality, Keats is now one with Nature, rejoicing in his own immortality. "He is a portion of the loveliness / Which once he made more lovely; he doth bear / His part, while the one Spirit's plastic stress / Sweeps through the dull dense world." So thorough is the transformation of mourning into joyous celebration that Shelley ultimately looks on his death as the promise of reunion with his beloved friend. "Why linger, why turn back, why shrink, my Heart? . . . 'Tis Adonis calls! oh, hasten thither, / No more let Life divide what Death can join together." ✹

Critical Views on
"Adonais"

[Neil Arditi is the author of "Shelley's 'Adonais' and the
Literary Canon." In the excerpt below from his article,
Arditi discusses Shelley's poem as a response to the critics of
John Keats, expressing a hope that the conservative literary
tradition will be open to reforming itself.]

To appreciate fully the impact of the death of John Keats on Shelley's
ideas about canon formation requires a considerable act of the
imagination. The reputation of Keats is now established; it no longer
shocks anyone to speak of him in the same breath as Milton. But the
shock would have been substantial to any contemporary reader of
Shelley's elegy for Keats, "Adonais." As Kenneth Neill Cameron
points out, Shelley's placement of Keats in the company of Homer,
Dante, and Milton "would have seemed ridiculous, indeed an insult
and a challenge, to conservative critics; and even to the most liberal
ones it would have seemed greatly exaggerated."

Shelley's desire to challenge conservative critics of Keats and his
own poetry is related to his conviction that Keats was killed by a
negative review of *Endymion*. That conviction has been frequently
derided, most notably by Lord Byron ("'Tis strange the mind, that
fiery particle,/Should let itself be snuff'd out by an article"). But
what matters more than Shelley's literalization of his own myth of
Keats's death is the myth itself, which should be read as a parable of
the vicissitudes of the canonical. ⟨...⟩

In "Adonais," Shelley considers the reaction of *The Quarterly
Review* to Keats's poetry in a similar light. Although John Wilson
Croker's infamous attack on Keats's *Endymion* spends much of its
time mocking the poet's craftsmanship, the critic's foremost
objection is bluntly put forward in the second paragraph of his
review: Keats "is unhappily a disciple of the new school of what has
been somewhere called Cockney poetry." In other words, Keats was a
member of the middle class with liberal sympathies and radical
friends like Leigh Hunt. The idea of such a figure striving for

canonicity struck Croker as absurd, for he accepted the canonical authority of Eton and Harrow, of Oxford and Cambridge, of the Church of England and the Tory party, and of *The Quarterly Review* itself, which was the literary mouthpiece of the conservative establishment. ⟨. . .⟩

"Adonais" does not despair of the capacity of literary tradition to renew itself, although it perhaps despairs of everything else. In *The English Elegy*, Peter Sacks movingly associates the suicidal drive in "Adonais" with a refusal of the consolations of elegy, an unwillingness to invest value in the compensatory mediations of figurative language. Indeed, beneath the carefully wrought surfaces of Shelley's poem lies an uncompromising will—an impulse to overleap all bounds. I would hasten to add, however, that this impulse, which mounts throughout the final third of the poem, is inseparable from Shelley's enormous investment in the moment Eliot minimizes: the moment in which a new work opens up the canon. That moment is, technically speaking, posthumous, and Shelley rushes towards it in the apocalyptic finale of "Adonais." One is reminded of the fifth and final section of "Ode to the West Wind," to which Shelley directly alludes at the opening of his last stanza:

> The breath whose might I have invoked in song
> Descends on me; my spirit's bark is driven,
> Far from the shore, far from the trembling throng
> Whose sails were never to the tempest given . . .

Sacks observes that Shelley's conclusion is "profoundly disturbing," particularly when we remember, as we must, that Shelley died a year later at sea, "refusing to follow a passing crew's advice to strike his sail during the storm." Others, like Earl Wasserman and Stuart Curran, have stressed the triumphant tone of the poem, precisely where it seems most suicidal. This paradox, in both "Ode to the West Wind" and "Adonais," is related to the phenomenon of self-canonization. One feels as if the author were dying into eternal life, or not dying at all, but being translated directly, like Enoch and Elijah, into a lasting presence.

What is disclosed at the moment of canonization? Nothing less, for Shelley, than the poetic nature of reality. By opening the canon to fresh revelation, a new poet disrupts the established order, recreating the past in his or her own image. What we took for granted, what we considered natural, necessary, realistic, traditional, authoritative, standard, and eternal is thereby altered. For the newly canonized poet has become one of the authors of our sense of reality. That is what Shelley means when he asserts that Keats "is made one with Nature," that his voice is heard "in all her music, from the moan/Of thunder, to the song of night's sweet bird." For a moment, we are inclined to think of reality as a poem to which Keats has contributed, to which Shelley is now contributing, and to which we too may contribute. In stanza 43, Shelley indulges to his fullest capacity this momentary inclination:

> he doth bear
> His part, while the one Spirit's plastic stress
> Sweeps through the dull dense world, compelling there,
> All new successions to the forms they wear;
> Torturing th'unwilling dross that checks its flight
> To its own likeness, as each mass may bear;
> And bursting in its beauty and its might
> From trees and beasts and men into the Heaven's light.

—Neil Arditi, "Shelley's 'Adonais' and the Literary Canon," *Raritan* 27, no. 1 (Summer 1997): pp. 125–27, 130–31.

PETER SACKS ON THE POEM AS A WORK OF MOURNING

[Peter Sacks is the author of *The English Elegy: Studies in the Genre from Spenser to Yeats* (1985) and *In These Mountains* (1986). In the excerpt below from his article, "Last Clouds: A Reading of *Adonais*," Sacks discusses the poem as a work of mourning and the ways in which Shelley has reworked the various literary sources upon which he relies.]

As is well known, Shelley described "Adonais" as "a highly wrought *piece of art*, perhaps better in point of composition than anything I have written." The poem's carefully "wrought" texture has made it particularly susceptible to close readings. Yet these readings, of which Earl Wasserman's has been the most comprehensive, have left ungauged the deepest level of the poem's complex movement. In some ways this is not surprising, for the objective of an elegy is, after all, to displace the urgent psychological currents of its work of mourning into the apparently more placid, aesthetically organized currents of language. Though elegies may weep, they must do so formally. They may not "break up their lines to weep" within that weeping.

In what follows, I shall try to go beyond a description of the form of "Adonais" to suggest how the pattern of its language relates to psychological and philosophical currents running deep within the poem. My questions include the following: What and how does Shelley mourn? How does he revise the inherited fictions of elegy? What is his relation to Urania? How does his narcissism affect the work of mourning? (This relation between narcissism and mourning, so carefully stressed by Freud, is noticeable in English elegies since the time of Spenser, and is of great importance to "Adonais.") What are the implications of the poem's extraordinary ending, and how does it relate to Shelley's ambivalence toward figurative language? Finally, how does this ambivalence, directed against the very fabric of the poem, relate specifically to the predicament of a mourner?

"Adonais" has two epigraphs. The first is a Greek couplet ascribed to Plato in the *Greek Anthology*. Following the common misattribution of the couplet to Plato the philosopher, Shelley translated these lines:

> Thou wert the morning star among the living,
> Ere thy fair light had fled;–
> Now, having died, thou art as Hesperus, giving
> New splendour to the dead.

Besides drawing attention to the stellar imagery of consolation, Shelley's choice of the epigraph indicates his desire to believe in a poetry somehow compatible with Platonic thought. ⟨. . .⟩

The second epigraph quotes the lines in Moschus's elegy for Bion, referring to the poet's having been poisoned by some insensitive scorner of verse. Shelley will return to this in stanza 36, elaborating his theory about Keats's death. While stressing the accusation's relevance to the poem, the epigraph foregrounds Shelley's debt to the Alexandrian elegy at large. The debt is immediately apparent in the opening line, which reads almost as a translation of Bion's lament for Adonis:

> I weep for Adonais—he is dead!
> O weep for Adonais! though our tears

> Thaw not the frost which binds so dear a head!
> And thou, sad Hour, selected from all years
> To mourn our loss, rouse thy obscure compeers,
> And teach them thine own sorrow, say: "With me
> Died Adonais; till the Future dares
> Forget the Past, his fate and fame shall be
> An echo and a light unto eternity!"

The first difference from Bion is of course the name Adonais, blending those of the vegetation deity, Adonis, and the Judaic Adonai. As historians of religion have shown, the originally physical significance of the fertility gods was allegorized and spiritualized by successive cults; and elegists, too, have continually revised the meaning of this most crucial figure of the genre. It is especially intriguing to note how Shelley has conserved the original figure within the new, for the poem itself unfolds the very *process* of resignification, moving from natural, sexual referents, towards their spiritualized successors. Shelley's act of renaming neatly suggests his intention to use and yet alter the inherited elegiac tradition: to use its essential strategy of assimilating the deceased to a figure of immortality, while redefining the meaning of that figure.

A second difference declares itself at once: unlike Bion, Shelley turns immediately to question the efficacy of weeping. By so doing, he begins a long interrogation of conventional gestures and figures of mourning. This oddly skeptical employment of conventions marks this poem as a true heir of "Lycidas" and "Astrophel," whose obsessions with "false surmise" and "verses vaine" had driven them to carefully persuasive consolations. As our reference to the "Plato" epigraph hinted, and as the poem will in fact show, Shelley's struggle with his legacy and with his very medium itself is particularly vexed. We can perhaps see this in the unusual prematurity with which he initiates the self-questioning or self-qualifying mode. Spenser had at least gathered momentum before examining the vanity of verse. And although Milton did begin with a self-doubting admission of sour immaturity, he at least did not suspect the "meed of some melodious tear."

Shelley's struggle to begin his work of mourning is further apparent in his deliberate *delegation* of such work to various figures throughout the opening sections of the poem. In fact it is not until quite far into the poem that Shelley moves beyond these delegate-mourners to assume a more personal voice. The delegates have at least two functions: they are all inadequate mourners, allowing Shelley to criticize them and to distance himself from various forms of unsuccessful grieving; and yet they keep his poem in motion, giving it the processional character of traditional elegies, allowing it to achieve the self-purifying and self-surpassing ceremonies so important to the work of mourning.

—Peter Sacks, "Last Clouds: A Reading of 'Adonais,'" *Studies in Romanticism* 23, no. 3 (Fall 1984): pp. 379–82.

James A. W. Heffernan on the Myth of Keats's Death

[James A. W. Heffernan is the author of *The Re-Creation of Landscape: A Study of Wordsworth, Coleridge, Constable and Turner* (1984) and *Museum of Words: The Poetics of Ekphrasis from Homer to Ashbery* (1993). In the excerpt below from his article, "*Adonais:* Shelley's Consumption of Keats,'" Heffernan discusses the myth of Keats's death upon which the poem is premised, a myth, Heffernan contends, which Shelley himself created in part as a way of projecting his own fears onto the other poet.]

Adonais is remarkable not simply because it at once reflects and transforms the whole tradition of pastoral elegy from Moschus and Bion to Spenser and Milton, but also because its point of departure is a singularly strange story about the cause of Keats's death. No one now believes this story, but critics normally assume that Shelley did, that he simply took into his poem what had been given to him as a fact. The story that Keats's death was precipitated by a harsh review of *Endymion* provides, says Ross Woodman, the "literal or historical level" on which Shelley builds his visionary poem. But when the "literal or historical level" is itself a piece of fiction, it should be much more thoroughly examined than it has been up to now. Careful scrutiny will show that Shelley himself invented the strange story of Keats's death. It will also allow us to see that in generating *Adonais* from that story, Shelley consumes as well as re-creates the personality of Keats.

The difficulty of isolating that personality from Shelley's version of it—or vision of it—is illustrated by Earl Wasserman's observation that "the skeletal form of the Adonis legend provided a nearly exact means of translating Keats's biography into a conceptual pattern." In one sense Wasserman is right. The story of a promising young poet slain by the malice of critics could be readily translated into the story of the youthful Adonis slain by an evil beast. But when Wasserman speaks of the poem as a translation of Keats's "biography," to what biography does he refer? In the spring of 1821, when Shelley wrote *Adonais*, there was none worthy of the name. There were merely a few facts and a number of rumors, and it was Shelley himself who created the most notorious rumor of all. Careful examination of the evidence will reveal that, beyond any reasonable doubt, the strange story of Keats's assassination is merely the first of the fictions with which Shelley deliberately consumed the facts of Keats's life.

This particular fiction was based on a purely second-hand knowledge of Keats's last years. The last that Shelley ever saw of Keats was in the winter of 1818, three years before his death. In July 1820, when Shelley was in Pisa, a letter from John Gisborne brought him news that Keats had burst a blood vessel and was seriously ill with consumption. When Shelley then wrote solicitously to Keats and invited him to come to Pisa, Keats sent his thanks, but indicated that he might not be able to come, and in fact never did come, going instead to Rome, where he died on February 23, 1821. In place of himself he asked John and Maria Gisborne to bring Shelley his words: a letter and the newly published volume of his poems—*Lamia, Isabella, The Eve of St. Agnes and Other Poems.* Yet it was not from Keats's words that Shelley constructed his version of Keats's ending. On the one hand, with no authorization from Keats, the publishers' "Advertisement" to the new volume apologized for the unfinished state of *Hyperion* by saying that "the reception given to [*Endymion*] discouraged the author from proceeding." On the other hand, Gisborne's letter told Shelley that Keats had burst a blood vessel. After Keats's death, this piece of information gave Shelley the means to literalize the metaphor merely implied by the "Advertisement": the criticism of *Endymion* had killed not merely Keats's ambition, but Keats himself. ⟨. . .⟩

Even before *Adonais* was published, Byron saw that Shelley's story about Keats—if true—showed him to be little more than a feckless narcissist: a man of "inordinate self-love" and without, Byron clearly implies, "powers of *resistance*." The crucial question raised by the Preface to *Adonais*, then, is why Shelley paints this picture: why does he slander Keats in the very act of seeking to defend him against slander? ⟨...⟩

Shelley also wished to project onto Keats the vulnerability he felt in himself, and thus to resolve the profound ambivalence with which he regarded the delicacy of his own idealism. The ambivalence is evident in poems such as "Ode to the West Wind," where the speaker represents himself as both the pathetically fragile victim of a crucifying world ("I fall upon the thorns of life! I bleed!") and as the resounding voice of a "Spirit fierce," a spirit "tameless, and swift, and proud." In *Adonais* itself, Shelley presents himself among the mourners as a "frail Form," a dying lamp, a falling shower, a breaking billow, a bacchant holding the thyrsus with a weak and shaking hand, and a stricken deer—in short, as "a Power / Girt round with weakness." Yet as Ross Woodman has recently argued, this picture of helpless vulnerability is not so much an idealized self-portrait as the parody of a posture which Shelley seeks to shed. ⟨...⟩

From the weeping of the first stanza to the lowering wind of the last one, the inexorable flow of the poem has carried its subject, its speaker, and even itself to the brink of annihilation. Up to the very last word, the present tense verbs of the final stanza signify passing and imminent absence rather than presence: the breath descends; I am driven; I am borne; the soul beacons. Yet even as the *I* who writes helplessly transcribes the imminence of its own passing, the eye of the I foresees its transformation into something eternally individuated and eternally present, as fixed as existential prediction can make it. An abode where the eternal *are* is a place where Keats and Shelley may individually co-exist—so long as the words which signify that abode remain alive and unconsumed.

—James A. W. Heffernan, "*Adonais:* Shelley's Consumption of Keats," *Studies in Romanticism* 23, no. 3 (Fall 1984): pp. 295–97, 301, 302, 315.

[In the excerpt below Daniel Wilson argues that the poem is
not an elegy but rather conforms to Shelley's definition of
drama in his *Defence of Poetry*. Wilson locates *Adonais*'s true
generic identity as a play in which the poet functions as an
amateur director and the reader assumes the dual part of
spectator and actor.]

Traditionally, Shelley's *Adonais* has been identified as a sustained
lyric in which a single, unitary voice identifiable as Shelley's moves
through lament to consolation and beckons towards some sort of
lyric transcendence through the dissolution of identity in the final
stanza. I would contend that *Adonais* more closely corresponds to
Shelley's description of drama in the *Defence of Poetry* and therefore
is better understood as a dramatic lyric. As such, the poem mediates
tensions between historical specificity and the impulse towards lyric
transcendence which destabilize the conception of the poem as a
monologic unity. The poem is literally a *play* of voices which enacts
Shelley's desire for lyric transcendence and poetic acceptance in a
self-reflexive dramatic lyric that functions according to Shelley's
conception of the best drama. In the *Defence* Shelley describes
drama that "continues to express poetry" as "a prismatic and many-
sided mirror, which collects the brightest rays of human nature and
divides and reproduces them from the simplicity of these
elementary forms, and touches them with majesty and beauty, and
multiplies all that it reflects." These tensions, and the dialogizing
effect of fragmenting the authorial subject within a self-drama,
posit the final totalizing identity not inside the poem, but outside,
as an auteur directing a play. The reader is consequently involved as
both spectator and actor in the play of identity. [I invoke the image
of the cinematic auteur for a number of reasons. First, as a
directorial model it is appropriate to the conception of *Adonais* as a
drama. Secondly, it is a figure which at once acknowledges the
authorial function as an overdetermined, "already written" legal and
economic entity, and yet allows for a subjective agency—Andrew
Sarris embarrassingly called it the "*élan* of the soul"—which
manipulates the preexisting available resources and limitations of
both industry and genre in order to impress vision and meaning on
exterior form.]

This tension between the historical and lyric impulses is inscribed in the very title and sub-title. The counterpointing between *Adonais* and *An Elegy on the Death of John Keats, Author of Endymion, Hyperion, Etc.* at once calls attention to the historical specificity of the poem and its desire for lyric transcendence. The subtitle and the narrative voice in the preface foreground the "time, place, circumstance, cause and effect" of the poem and pre(in)scribe its referents by asking the reader to identify Adonais as John Keats and the principal voices of lament and consolation in the poem as the single, evolving voice of Shelley. Such identification invites the reader to identify *with* Shelley's grief and outrage at Keats's death at the hands of the critic in the *Quarterly Review*. Conversely, the title and the elegiac conventions of the poem function to remove the utterance from the historical circumstances of its composition and from the occasion for Shelley's personal grief by trying to universalize that grief, turning it into one of the "unchangeable forms of human nature." These conventions and the designation of "elegy" in the subtitle further jeopardize the reader's identification with Shelley's grief, either real or idealized, by asserting the poem's status as what Shelley calls "a highly wrought *piece of art*." To assert the aestheticization of the utterance is to proclaim the artifice of the elegiac voices, destabilize the readers' identification of the historical Shelley with those voices, and undermine our acceptance of or identification with the effusions of grief and transcendence in the lament and consolation. We are forced to see in Shelley's poem the same difficulties Samuel Johnson saw in Milton's *Lycidas*: it mixes the "trifling fictions" of convention with the "sacred truths" of lyric and makes us suspect that "where there is leisure for fiction there is little grief."

We may also resist identifying the lyric voices in the poem as Shelley's when we consider his narrative manipulations in the preface. There he asserts that he is "an impartial judge" of Keats's poetry and yet asserts his bias that Keats was "among the writers of the highest genius" to adorn the age. But both concepts of partiality and impartiality are integral to the text. Shelley must announce his partiality in order to justify and lend an historical referent to the lament: indeed the lament and the poem itself are a *de facto* admission of partiality. But his assumption of an impartial role in the preface is an important rhetorical strategy that allows Shelley to valorize his own critical perception at the expense of the "savage criticism" of the "wretched men" who write for the *Quarterly Review*. More precisely, it is a strategy that allows Shelley to create the illusion of difference between his evaluation and that expressed in the *Quarterly Review* and enables him to create the narration of Keats's death that becomes the fictitious "historical" pretext of the poem.

In "*Adonais*: Shelley's Consumption of Keats," James Heffernan traced the evolution of Shelley's fabrication of the apocryphal story of Keats's death. He argues that the narrative of Keats's death and the consequential figuring of Keats as a weak young flower blighted by such an insubstantial frost allows Shelley to "consume Keats in a myth of his own making." Quite frankly, Shelley fakes the circumstances of Keats's death so he can stage the scenes of his own equally faked outrage and grief. Keats's corpse becomes a prop around which Shelley demonstrates his own poetic power. If Heffernan's argument is correct—he builds a very convincing case— then the lyricism of the poem does not have *real* personal and historical referents, but instead signifies only its own enactment on the stage of referentiality. The poem thus is not an expression of grief or desire for lyric transcendence but a *performance* of poetical skill.

> —Daniel Wilson, "'Applaud the Deed': The Theatre of Lyricism in Shelley's *Adonais*," *The Wordsworth Circle* 25, no. 1 (Winter 1994): pp. 10–11.

MARTHA BANTA ON OCCULT IMAGERY

[Martha Banta is the author of *Imaging American Women: Idea and Ideals in Cultural History* (1987) and *Taylored Lives: Narrative Productions in the Age of Taylor, Veblen and Ford* (1993). In the excerpt below, Banta discusses occult imagery of the poem and in so doing moves between two traditionally antithetical modes of art versus science in order to explain its aesthetic qualities.]

In terms of what might be called "the critics' sublime" there is ever the question of how we as scholar-interpreters are to deal in any reasoned way with mysteries considered unfathomable by the human imagination. If the material under review is, say, a poem, literary critics such as Harold Bloom will scorn the contemptible notion of giving recognition to the occult—that Harlot Mystery protective of the secret knowledge and power it denies to mankind at large. To Bloom in *The Visionary Company*, Blake's vital iconoclasm is arrayed against the drift by Coleridge into "orthodox babbling," and fiery humanism's intuitions are triumphant over the enslaving obscurantism of both cold reason and darkling superstition. If we shift from art to science in order to try to assess the legitimacy of the scientific responses to the occult, we meet with scathing remarks about the "irresponsible and trendy academicians" currently cluttering up the history of science by efforts to link the discoveries of true scientists with the dabblings of alchemists. Think, then, what risks are involved when the attempt is made—as I shall here—to take up a particular problem in the occult which requires movements between art (the painting and the poem) and science (the study of pure light and prismatic color) in order to come nearer to the aesthetics, physics, and metaphysics of the sublime—drawing all these considerations through the fine mesh of that sieve we call Romanticism.

Turner and Shelley (with Blake as their foil) are the leading human figures of this paper, but the conceptions and visualizations of the sun form its true center. The specific images to which I shall refer are these: the poet-Self at the end of "Adonais" leaping through the dome of many-colored glass into the high white purity of the Ideal; the aureoled Human Form Divine celebrating the "Glad Day" of its self-fulfillment; the imperious "Angel Standing in the Sun" dissolving the sky and our hearts in awesome manifestation of the Unknowable. These images, and these questions of crucial moment to the Romantic mind: Is the sun to be approached in terms of vision (optics) or the visionary (intuition)? Is its meaning restricted to the coterie of occultists or thrown open to the inquiries of the newly accredited sciences? Is its blaze of light the final revelation by which the human imagination is to be freed or the ultimate mystery by which the craving for omniscience and omnipotence will be frustrated?

Sir David Brewster, Fellow of the Royal Society of Edinburgh, was a lifelong student of optics whose treatises on light and color were frequently consulted by Turner. In 1832, Brewster opened the argument of *Letters on Natural Magic, addressed to Sir Walter Scott, Bart.* by denouncing (as had Blake and Shelley) the "spiritual despotism" by which "The prince, the priest, and the sage" acted through possession of esoteric knowledge of chemistry, drugs, astronomy, and optics "to deceive and enslave their species. . . ." Yet, Brewster is pleased to declare, contemporary science can now look back upon what the ancients called impenetrable mysteries to detect in them man's first discoveries of the natural origins of all earthly events. ⟨. . .⟩

If the Romantic artist had to consider the effects upon his vision of the stance he took between science (demonstrable laws we can know by our own efforts) and the occult (divine mysteries we may never have disclosed to us), he had also to contend with that knot of feelings associated with the sublime; he had to decide the degree to which the mind forbids or furthers its awareness of how and why the great sun lights up the heavens. In 1832, Sir David Brewster insisted that scientific knowledge in league with religious feeling puts an end to terror in the face of the sun's powers. But there were those who said that religion without terror is a self-contradiction, while the science that knows no tightening of the heart over its perceptions of the vast, wild, essentially ungovernable forces abroad in the universe—no better represented than by the sun's blaze—is no true science. Thomas Weiskel in his finely provocative book on the Romantic Sublime defines it as that which transcends the human— that "ultimacy" lying beyond our capacity to come to any complete comprehension of its being or its purpose. Marked by infinity and eternity, *larger* and *longer* than human measurements can fathom, such a sense of "more" requires, as Weiskel argues, a god-term. By the eighteenth century, "light" or "sun" had become preeminently the term by which men tried to express the overwhelming experience that came to them as they witnessed the material fact of inexplicable power. Whether the origins and purposes of that power, and the reasons why it could so stir the mind, would remain forever hidden or could be discovered to human understanding was the issue. However uneasy the Romantics of agnostic inclination may have been over orthodox justifications for the mystery of "ultimacy"—an unease that makes the Romantic Sublime different from the more serene experience declared by Akenside, Addison, Young, and Burke—they had to deal with the fact that, as Weiskel puts it, there is "no way to keep the sublime closed to 'mystical' explanations"; the influx of energy that sets the soul soaring may well come from "some suprapersonal reservoir which cannot be refuted or verified." ⟨...⟩

The scholarship on Shelley has had much to say about his concerns with science, occultism, the ideal, the sublime, the hopes he placed in the power of the imagination to rise above the mundanity of nature and of life, and the extreme frustrations he experienced over its limits. There is no lack of evidence concerning Shelley's continual, and varied, examination of light as a metaphor for the unknowable. But in whatever direction Shelley turned, he could not be consoled. Rather than submission, he often felt the rage of his frustration before the sealed door of the unknown—rage, and also the guilt and anxieties that slew the confidence of the "sensibility poets" of whom Weiskel writes and among whom I number Shelley. Rage, guilt, anxieties, the inability to live at ease in this world, and the occasional urge to move into the de-creating glory of death—this is how Harold Bloom in *The Visionary Company* reads the poetic voice in "Adonais" of 1821 in which the speaker vanishes, absorbed by the same baffling mysteries he had once eagerly aspired to break open.

—Martha Banta, "Adonais and the Angel: Light, Color, and the Occult Sublime," *The Wordsworth Circle* 8, no. 2 (Spring 1977): pp. 113, 115–16.

BARRY MAGARIAN ON SHELLEY'S REWORKING OF THE ELEGIAC GENRE

[In the following excerpt, Barry Magarian discusses the poem in terms of an elegy, a poem memorializing a deceased person, and the number of ways in which it contradicts conventional expectations of that genre.]

Adonais's (1821) treatment of death makes the poem peculiarly provisional in terms of its emotional and intellectual outlook. The subject of death is initially one that fosters a mood of consolatory lamentation. It ends by precipitating and pressing forward a view of imaginative and spiritual liberation. The latter view is intimately connected with the glimpse the poem offers at the end of a higher vision that apparently signals a harmonious union with Adonais while also suggesting a demonic force that, in itself, is at odds with harmony. Such duality, both in the fact of the changing perceptions of death that the poem offers, and in the simultaneously harmonious and demonic vision of life beyond the grave, accounts for the poem's difficulty. The poem, like all pastoral elegies, begins by grieving for the loss of a life but ends, unlike other elegies, by grieving for life itself and insisting on the need to get beyond its distorting veil ('Life, like a dome of many-coloured glass, / Stains the white radiance of Eternity'). It, like *The Triumph of Life* (1822), conveys a sense of life as the progenitor of a process of victimization and disfiguration. The poem is indeterminate because it vividly recreates this sense of life as a *cul de sac* that stifles, as opposed to enlarges, imaginative and spiritual possibilities, while suggesting a solution—an entry into a higher realm—that may be merely an act of pragmatic escapism. *Adonais* strains to reach toward a solution to the problem of loss and bereavement. Such straining lifts the poem into realms of the imagination, while also confronting both Shelley and the reader with a sceptical and comfortless view of the problem of death. ⟨...⟩

Keats's death was the immediate trigger to the writing of the poem. The enduring legacy of Keats's poetry is acknowledged by the various allusions to it which serve the function of suggesting Keats's literary presence and this, in turn, parallels the gradual articulation of the fact of his presence in nature later on in the poem. The volume of 1820 entitled *Lamia, Isabella, The Eve of St. Agnes, and other poems* has a prominent place in Shelley's mind. The poems in this volume were the ones most admired by Shelley.

In Ross Woodman's words, *Adonais* 'concerns the plight of the visionary in a society controlled by tyrannical forces.' Shelley felt himself to be such a figure and consequently the writing of the poem provided an opportunity to mourn his own, as well as Keats's fate.

The personal edge to the work is foreshadowed in early drafts of the Preface, later cancelled by Shelley on the advice of John Taaffe. Here Shelley self-deceptively tries to make nonchalant his own disappointment with the way in which he has been received by the literary establishment: 'I will allow myself a first and last word on the subject of calumny as it relates to me.' Shelley also paints a picture of a fatalistic reclusiveness that has been forced upon him: 'As a man, I shrink from notice and regard; the ebb and flow of the world vexes me; I desire to be left in peace.' ⟨. . .⟩

Implicit in the following extract is the sense of death as release: 'it would be one subject less for regret, to me, it I could consider my death as no irremediable misfortune to you' (To Claire Clairmont, 14 May 1821). The last two extracts point to *Adonais*'s obsession with death as a means with which to escape 'the ebb and flow of the world' (from the cancelled Preface), or, in the poem's terms, 'the contagion of the world's slow stain.' This concentration on death leads, in Richard Holmes's view, to a problem: 'The poem seeks to celebrate the indestructible life of the creative spirit, in art and in nature; yet its personal drive and its most intense images tend towards consummation and death.' This, however, is an oversimplified view in that it fails to take into account the poem's altering conceptions of death. It is, after all, the transformation of the perception of death from an initial image of destructiveness to one of liberation undercut by a different kind of destructiveness— that of wilful abandon to the elements—which gives the poem its power.

Another difficulty with the poem is whether it proceeds in a linear fashion. Is Shelley's awareness of his ending apparent at the start of the poem, and if it is, does that not make the sense of the poem as a voyage of discovery, in some way, redundant? ⟨. . .⟩

It is important to bear in mind that Shelley's poem can only give the illusion of happening in time. By virtue of the fact that it is so carefully wrought and orchestrated it immediately suggests a painstaking artifice and completedness that has no equivalent in real time and, by implication, real life. The poem exists as a whole and should be read as such, with an awareness of its ongoing and fluid structure. This position has been carefully and comprehensively articulated by Earl Wasserman. His main argument is that *Adonais* proceeds by virtue of the fact that each of its movements provide a successive redefinition of the central concerns and themes of what has gone before so that the poem only comes into its own right by its end, at which time it has been fitted into a wider thematic and imaginative context. This argument illustrates how the poem must be read both with an awareness of its *whole* structure—so much of a piece is the poem—but also with a sense of its ongoing fluidity. Like Adonais himself who is continually being redefined and transmuted into other reincarnations, the poem is also moulding itself into successive realisations of its own meaning. The movement by which these various modes are effected is very carefully wrought. *Adonais* adheres to the formal precision of the pastoral elegy and wants to impose strict order on the chaos of grief. However, the poem's emotion is eventually of a kind that is more heartfelt and acute than formal and reserved and this signals a radical departure from, say, the strictly impersonal elegies of Bion and Moschus. The final third of the poem is a display of rhetorical rapture that suggests that the poet has glimpsed into a world whose engulfingness goes hand in hand with such rapture.

—Barry Magarian, "The Indeterminacy of Shelley's *Adonais:* Liberation and Destruction," *The Keats-Shelley Review* 9 (Spring 1995): pp. 15, 16–19.

Thematic Analysis of
"The Triumph of Life"

Written in the early summer of 1822, Shelley left "The Triumph of Life" unfinished when he died on July 8, 1822, when his boat *Don Juan* capsized. Indeed, Shelley had written part of the poem while sailing in this very same boat.

Earlier in that same fateful year, feeling restless amid his circle of friends at Pisa and irritated by the company of the sardonic Byron, Shelley had the plan to divert his attention to amateur theatricals; he even planned to act in *Othello*. Though this never came to pass, Shelley continued to be interested in drama. He also became infatuated with Jane Williams, the common-law wife of his friend Edward, while he shared a summer rental with Edward and Jane. The Casa Magni, near Lerici, was set amid the romantic surroundings of a steep and thickly wooded hillside. In Jane, Shelley found spiritual relief during times of torment or melancholy. He also enjoyed the beauty of her singing, and she was the inspiration for a series of poems Shelley addressed to her, "[t]he best and brightest / . . . Fairer far than this fair day." The first of this series is "To Jane. The Invitation," and in it Shelley adopts a relaxed tone that speaks of romantic love in a calm and even voice he would incorporate into his final poem.

"The Triumph of Life" is a poem whose structure bears some resemblance to the medieval genre of the dream-vision, an allegory or story containing moral and religious significance though embedded within a more obvious narrative tale. Its common elements include a poet who falls asleep in an idyllic scene, a garden or pleasant wood, lulled by the soothing sounds of Nature, dreaming of real people or symbolic actions, which, upon waking, will be memorable and laden with profound significance. Stated in another way, the dream-vision can be the story of the poet's psychological journey, a dream that begins in great confusion and ends with a vision of perfect harmony. Although "The Triumph of Life" does not strictly conform to the medieval genre, this genre does provide a framework for understanding the fantastic imagery conjured up by a "dreaming" poet caught up in a "trance of wondrous thought."

Additionally, there is yet another medieval element in the poem: the notion of a pageant or celebration, although for Shelley it exists as a sham imitation, "the just similitude / Of a triumphal pageant." "The Triumph of Life" holds many images of pageants, and the word *pageant* itself derived from the medieval Latin word *pagina*, which referred to the stage or platform for open air-performances of mystery plays; this platform was mounted on wheels so that it could be moved from town to town.

The poem also takes its name from poems of the medieval poet Petrarch called *Trionfi*. This word is from the Latin *triumphus*, referring to the ceremonial entrance of a victorious general into ancient Rome, followed by a procession, through the "sacred" gates (*porta triumphalis*) that were barred to all others. The procession often led to the temple of Jupiter on the Capitol, and it would also include the general's prisoners of war. Essentially, it was made up of the *triumphator*, dressed in costume, on a four-horse chariot, accompanied by outriders, displaying the spoils of war, the army, and the animals for sacrifice. The entire senate and all the magistrates were supposed to escort this entourage; the right to triumph was dependent on a vote of the people, granting permission for the general to retain his army in the city. However, in the late republics, the original rules were bent by the influence of political power and soon became the monopoly of the emperor.

Other interpretations of the word triumph within "The Triumph of Life" are simply *procession* or *victory*, and for Shelley the word may denote humanity's victory over Nature and the restraints and struggles of mortal existence. Or perhaps this poem uses an ironic application of the word triumph, for the frenzied crowd has in fact no cause to celebrate.

In the beginning lines of the poem (the first 40), we are presented with an energized scene, unlike the sweetness and repose of its medieval prototype, in which nature fully partakes of the festivities: "Swift as a spirit hastening to his task . . . the Sun sprang forth, / Rejoicing in his splendour, and the mask / Of darkness fell from the awakened Earth." This is hardly a setting for midday dreaming but rather a boisterous awakening from a sleeping state, summoning all to the temple to participate in the ceremonial rites. "The smokeless altars of the mountain snows / Flamed above crimson clouds," and the flowers themselves quivered from the excitement as they "unclose / Their trembling eyelids to the kiss of day."

Nevertheless, the sensuousness of the scene also contains suggestions of something far more sacred in its Christian overtones: "Rise as the Sun their father rose, to bear / Their portion of the toil which he of old / Took as his own and then imposed on them." Thus we understand that the poet is implying a significance far deeper than the sensual indulgence of the opening lines. Despite all the pageantry, his dream-like vision begins at line 29, "[w]hen a strange trance over my fancy grew / Which was not slumber, for the share it spread / Was so transparent that the scene came through." This trance strangely transforms the earlier noise into a quieter scene, incorporating some of the elements of its medieval prototype: "[A]nd heard as there / The birds, the fountains and the Ocean hold / Sweet talk in music through the enamoured air."

However, this quieting of nature serves as the prelude to another unexpected shock, for next we are transported, along with the poet, into a nightmarish procession, "thick strewn with summer dust, and a great stream / Of people . . . Numerous as gnats upon the evening gleam" with the strange and foreboding message of imminent death, "with steps towards the tomb," of young and old, made equal by the terrible sight. "Mixed in one might torrent did appear. / Some flying from the thing they feared and some / Seeking the object of another's fear." The poet hints that some are stricken by the unrelieved solitariness of narcissistic preoccupation and misguided quest. Most importantly and perhaps most terrible, similar to Dante's *Inferno*, all those who are caught up in this breathless procession are condemned to an enervating waste of energy, so much so that they appear doomed to futile pursuit of that which they can never hope to attain. "Old men and women foully disarrayed / Shake their grey hair in the insulting wind . . . To reach the car of light which leaves them still." Indeed, "The Triumph of Life" rehearses a variety of images, all of which underscore the theme of exhaustion and fruitless effort.

Presiding over this procession, which "throng grew wilder, as the woods of June / When the South wind shakes the extinguished day—," is a frightening chariot piloted by a deformed Shape, "[b]eneath a dusky hood and double cape, Crouching within the shadow of a tomb," a messenger of death himself who can hardly be trusted as a spiritual guide. He is a "Janus-visaged Shadow," like the Roman god represented on the gates of the city, who looks both ways, before and after, only this Shadowy charioteer has four faces, all of which are blindfolded, carried along at a breathless and unavailing speed. The entourage shackled to that chariot are those who have abused their power, as "imperial Rome poured forth her living sea." The chariot bears "a captive multitude . . . all those who had grown old in power / Or misery,—all who have their aged subdued, / By action or by suffering." This motley crew, representatives of a depraved earthly existence, is contrasted with the sacred few who had the wisdom and the spiritual understanding to reject the empty trappings of worldly power. "All but the sacred few who could not tame / Their spirits to the Conqueror . . . As soon / As they had touched the world with living flame / Fled back like eagles to their native noon."

As Shelley is observing "this sad pageantry," he asks himself just what this motley crew of shadowy figures is really all about. The answer he receives is "Life," from a "grim Feature" who offers to explain all the events that have taken place since morning. This grim figure is none other than Jean-Jacques Rousseau, a French philosopher, writer, and political theorist whose writings inspired the French Revolution and influenced the Romantic writers. He was an important influence on Shelley in that he was a radical thinker, speaking out against religious dogma in favor of a more individual and emotional response toward God; he also endorsed complete political freedom for all people. In this poem, he is Shelley's guide, a wise but somewhat "fallen" figure who cannot even save himself.

One of the most important aspects of Rousseau's thinking we see in "The Triumph of Life," which advocates moderation of the emotions, is the concept that the emotions are vital to relationships of love and friendship. Indeed, Rousseau's famous autobiographical *Confessions* recounts his own youthful excesses: "Corruption would not now thus much inherit / Of what was once Rousseau—nor this disguise / Stain that within which still disdains to wear it.—" Thus, Rousseau's life serves as an example of the misguided celebrants who are "tortured by the agonizing pleasure" that results from over-indulgence in those sensuous pleasures that lead them "[o]ft to new bright destruction." Yet the lesson Rousseau is most anxious to teach Shelley concerns the abuse of power, an abuse that stems from people not truly understanding themselves or their motivations and impulses. In that lack of understanding, they fail to able to distinguish desire and virtue. "And much I grieved to think how power and will / In opposition rule our mortal day / And why God made irreconcilable / Good and the means of good." Most important of all is the fact that Rousseau does not forget to include himself in the list of those whose efforts have been perverted, whose talents were wasted, or whose focus was lead astray. He assigns culpability to himself for having indiscriminately and immoderately given in to his desires, unlike "[t]he great bards of old who only quelled / The passions." His voice comes to us from a poem predicated on the need to moderate the emotions and respect the physical limitations of human existence. "'I was overcome / By my own heart alone, which neither age / Nor tears nor infamy nor now the tomb / Could temper to its object.'" Neither was he able to distinguish between those of true worth and false demagogues: "'I desire to worship those who drew / New figures on its false and fragile glass / As the old faded.'" "'Figures ever new / Rise on the bubble.'"

Yet, for all of Rousseau's failings, he was a man of great vision and high hopes for humanity, and the same motivating spirit of his younger days remains invincible, rendering him fit to serve as Shelley's counselor in this sad parade of lost souls. For Rousseau, himself a former participant in this "mock" pageant, "I among the multitude / Was swept; me sweetest flowers delayed not long, / . . . but among / The thickest billows of the living storm / I plunged." Therefore, we should not be surprised that his spirit, even in retrospect, remains indomitable till the very end. For there is, at least in Rousseau's thinking, a mitigating circumstance, if not a redemptive principle, within his own history—namely, love and unfailing loyalty to his heart's desires.

Although "The Triumph of Life" ends on a note of fatalism regarding the human condition, it still offers the chance to recoup a type of spirituality by remaining faithful to one's hopes and aspirations. Despite the fact that there is pain and suffering, one needs to be fully responsive to all life's circumstances. Though referring specifically to Dante, Rousseau's message is universal. "Of him who from the lowest depths of Hell / Through every Paradise and through all glory / Love led serene, and who returned to tell . . . How all things are transfigured, except Love." ❀

Critical Views on
"The Triumph of Life"

KAREN A. WEISMAN ON THE ELUSIVE NATURE OF TRUTH

[Karen A. Weisman is the author of *Imageless Truths: Shelley's Poetic Fictions* (1994). In the excerpt below from her article, "Shelley's Triumph of Life over Fiction," Weisman addresses the poem's final question: What is life in our mundane experience of the world? She concludes that the poem ends in a tacit acknowledgment that any attempt to grasp the ultimate truth is but another fiction.]

The title that Shelley gave to his final, unfinished poem is "The Triumph of Life," and the last question which the narrator asks in that poem is "Then, What is Life?" One of the central scenes concerns the figurative car of life vanquishing those who come into contact with it. ⟨. . .⟩ I would submit that "The Triumph of Life" takes both metaphysical dualism, and its inevitable epistemological doubt, as givens. Shelley is already fully convinced that the deep truth, as he has Demogorgon maintain in *Prometheus Unbound*, is imageless, is beyond even poetic imaging. Now, in his final year, he is preoccupied by poetry's relationship to quotidian existence, for he already acknowledges the inherent inefficacy of fiction and its tropes.

Indeed, in the opening situation of the poem, we are presented with a description of a natural, temporal phenomenon (sunlight), which is interrupted by a vision, and then a vision within vision, until the sequence returns to the unanswerable question: not, what is transcendence, but what is life, the quotidian existence which we continue to inhabit when our visionary quests have failed. The question could never have been successfully answered, because the poem is agonizingly aware of the triumph of life over poetic fiction; and Shelley could only illustrate this within the confines of a poetic fiction, an original myth which self-destructs even as it destroys. ⟨. . .⟩

By the time "The Triumph of Life" is written, then, Shelley is suspended between desire to ascent to some unknowable, other-worldly, ubiquitous One, and a conflicting desire to answer the question which he poses at the end of "Mont Blanc": if value inheres in the mountain only as it becomes an object to be troped upon, then what is the mountain as mountain? "The Triumph" picks up, then, where "Mont Blanc" ends and where *Adonais* fears to travel, as Shelley determines to explore the means by which human beings actually cope with the task of living. And to his horror, he discovers that the concept of life, in the sense even of quotidian existence, is as amorphous an abstraction, as resistant to definition, as are his notions of transcendence. For the purposes of this poem, "life" is construed as a coping with images—themselves doomed always to inefficacy—or as our experience of subject-object relationship. This epistemological/phenomenological perspective sees myth, or fiction, as the center of the subject-object dualism, as well as of the quite different natural-transcendent one. The existence (and failure) of the latter use of myth involves the failure of the former. We shall further see that since mythic structures make tropes out of objects, and since the visionary questor also appropriates objects as tropes of transcendence, life remains elusive, triumphant in its impenetrability. If troped objects can cease to exist *as* objects for the myth maker, and if we remain living anyway in a world progressively robbed by us, through our troping, of its components, then life ultimately overcomes us.

It is therefore entirely appropriate that the poem begins with a simile: "Swift as a spirit hastening to his task / Of glory and of good, the Sun sprang forth." Since "The Triumph" discloses Shelley's growing suspicion of the potential inefficacy and the danger of fiction and myth—or of fiction as hardened into myth—its initial association makes the associative leap, the conscious artifice, more obtrusive. ⟨...⟩

Lloyd Abbey voices the reader's initial and important response to such dilemmas: "The poem systematically posits image after image as potential analogue of ultimate reality and then, by submerging these images in life's natural cycle, poetically demonstrates their inadequacy. But if temporal metaphors are inadequate as vehicles to the transcendence of temporality, or even to the spiritualizing of temporality, what becomes of the external, empirical world from which those metaphors are drawn? The pursuit of shadows is analogous to the futile human pursuit of reality by way of fictions whose fictionality has been suppressed. In "The Triumph of Life," deferral of relationship with the sun obscures the sun and leaves clouds. Deferral of perception of the clouds—still objective objects—leaves the creator of tropes merely with shadows of clouds. But shadows are insubstantial stuff, and so after artifice obscures the sun and vision annihilates conscious perception of it, life makes its presence known by reasserting its own omnipresence—one which is forsaken by questors who seek a common denominator to existence. Since the narrator has already effectively diminished the sun, it is appropriate that it is the figurative light of life which makes him conscious of the sun's diminution: "And a cold glare, intenser than the noon / But icy cold, obscured with [ ] light / The Sun as he the stars." Just when they thought they were transcending life, it reappears to them in its full "light," reminding them that it is the light of common life in which they are bound to live.

—Karen A. Weisman, "Shelley's Triumph of Life over Fiction,"
Philological Quarterly 71, no. 3 (Summer 1992): pp. 337, 338–39, 342.

DAVID QUINT ON THE SIGNIFICANCE OF ROUSSEAU

[David Quint is the author of *Epic and Empire: Politics and Generic Form from Virgil to Milton* (1993) and *Montaigne and the Quality of Mercy: Ethical and Political Themes in the Essais* (1998). In the excerpt below from his article, "Representation and Ideology in *The Triumph of Life*," Quint discusses how both Rousseau and the triumphal procession are enslaved by their worship of representational images.]

Shelley's criticism of Dante mirrors his own larger concerns. The immense scope of Dante's poem attests to the stimulus of a love whose object the same poem cannot represent or "transfigure." Coextensive with the impulse of human love, the imagination is infinite; but the figures and words by which the imaginative experience expresses itself are finite. The free imagination is imprisoned by its very act of *shaping* or image-making, particularly when its images are derived from the historical ideologies ("words of hate and awe")—in Dante's case, Christianity. The human mind habitually ignores or accepts its imprisonment, and worships the shapes it or other, similar minds have created. ⟨...⟩

The deformation of the imaginative experience into ideology is both the subject and intrinsic poetic process of *The Triumph of Life*. The parodistic elements of the poem, Biblical, Platonic, Dantesque, epitomize its theme: "thought's empire over thought," a history of texts that forever recast the life of the mind into their own image. Criticism treating its allusive texture by reading backwards through the continuum of the history of ideas—the same continuum that is portrayed in the enslaved triumphal procession following the chariot of Life—understandably has not yielded satisfactory solutions to its difficulties; nor have recent studies which have re-allegorized its traditional literary *topoi*. We cannot dispense with either critical approach in a discussion of *The Triumph of Life*, yet both are apt to obscure Shelley's more radical intentions. His allegorical figures do not point to some paraphrasable abstraction for which they have been substituted, but to their own function as imaginative representation. The two major "allegories" of the poem, the theophanic chariot and the female soul-figure who appears to Rousseau, are derived from two central myths of Western civilization, and portray their own progress from representation to myth and their eventual ideological domination over the human mind. In both instances, Shelley reduces the representational image to its lowest common denominator, to mere "Shape."

The shadow, the mediation in Plato's cave of the philosopher, is taken over by Shelley as a general figure for representation. In the poem's terms, human shadows stand for the figures cast by the imagination, reflections not of the outer but of the inner man. These and other shadows haunt the crowd of humanity that attends the chariot of Life.

> And others mournfully within the gloom
>
> Of their own shadow walked, and called it death . . .
>   And some fled from it as it were a ghost,
> Half fainting in the affliction of vain breath.
>
>   But more with motions which each other crost
> Pursued or shunned the shadows the clouds threw
>   Or birds within the noonday ether lost,
>
> Upon that path where flowers never grew;

And weary with vain toil & faint for thirst
Heard not the fountains whose melodious dew

Out of their mossy cells forever burst
Nor felt the breeze which from the forest told
Of grassy paths, & wood lawns interspersed

With overarching elms & caverns cold,
And violet banks where sweet dreams brood, but they
Pursued their serious folly as of old . . .

Sight supersedes the other senses but in a negative mode; man's obsession with the visual shadow alienates him from the synesthetic sources of the imagination, the fountain and cave which reappear at the beginning of Rousseau's autobiographical narrative. The passage distinguishes two forms of shadow-worship. The private self-enchanters are possessed by their own shadows. The public ideologues, greater in number and prone to social discord ("with motions which each other crost"), pursue or shun shadows cast by foreign objects blocking the sun, like the "eclipse" which is worshipped in place of the "true Sun" in verses 288-292. While this distinction separates the individual poet, Rousseau, in love with his own imaginative creations, from the multitudes who follow the chariot as the victims of the historical ideologies, it is, in fact, a distinction without a difference. Rousseau, too, is swept up in the triumphal procession, and, his own claims to the contrary, he is an exemplary rather than an exceptional figure. His detailed narrative will reveal the common structure of desire which leads self-enchanter and ideologue alike into life-imprisonment by the representational image.

As representations of an inner subjectivity, Shelley implies in the *Essay on Love*, the human shadows wrought by the imagination project an absence no more substantial than the evanescent cloud or lost bird.

> Thou demandest, What is Love? It is that powerful attraction towards all that we conceive or fear, or hope beyond ourselves, when we find within our own thoughts the chasm of an insufficient void and seek to waken in all things that are a community with what we experience within ourselves.

The void within, an unconstituted selfhood, initiates the desire for external self-representation. The imagination turns to "all things that are" outside the self in search of a sympathetic kindred spirit or mirror image that will, in turn, gloss or define the self. The operative word here is "all." The hunger of the self, the "chasm," is infinite, and seeks an infinite object. This quest of love is as endless as it is vital to the human spirit: Shelley equates its cessation with a living death.

> So soon as this want or power is dead, man becomes the living sepulchre of himself, and what yet survives is the mere husk of what he once was.

Here is the subject matter of *The Triumph of Life*: a death-in-life occasioned by man's surrender to ideological representation, whether an ideology shaped by the private imagination or derived ready-made from past thinkers. Prisoners of their own mental constructs, the self-enchanters "mournfully within the gloom / Of their own shadow walked, and called it death." A similar "deep night" enveloped the ideologues behind the chariot during their lifetimes ("ere evening").

> "And who are those chained to the car?" "The Wise,
>
> "The great, the unforgotten: they who wore
>   Mitres & helms & crowns, or wreathes of light,
> Signs of thought's empire over thought; their lore
>
>   Taught them not this—to know themselves; their might
> Could not repress the mutiny within,
>   And for the morn of truth they feigned, deep night
>
> Caught them ere evening."

> —David Quint, "Representation and Ideology in *The Triumph of Life*," *Studies in English Literature 1500–1900* 18, no. 4 (Autumn 1978): pp. 639–42.

LINDA E. MARSHALL ON THE POEM'S COMPLEX IMAGERY OF LIGHT

[Linda E. Marshall is the author of "'Transfigured to His Likeness': Sensible Transcendentalism in Christian Rosetti's Later Life: A Double Sonnet of Sonnets" (1994) and "Astronomy of the Invisible: Contexts for Christina

Rossetti's Heavenly Parables" (1999). In the excerpt below from her article, "The 'Shape of All Light' in Shelley's *The Triumph of Life*," Marshall provides a critical overview concerning the identity of the figure of light in Rousseau's vision, arguing that it is the shape of Lucifer, the morning star, that is still present at sunrise.]

Rousseau's vision of the "shape all light" in Shelley's *The Triumph of Life* has been diversely interpreted. The shape herself is problematic: to some she is near kin to Intellectual Beauty or to the Witch of Atlas; to others she is the Rahab of deceptive Nature or the Iris of the distorting Imagination. Her role as Venus Pandemos, however, is one that few readers can accept, and for such critics as Butter and Reiman her ideality is blemished only by the extent to which they see her clouded by her participation in the natural world and in time. The unseduced, on the other hand, have more logical arguments to support their mistrust of the shape, since they may relate her seemingly maleficent potion to her deceptive charm. Those who persist in unqualified admiration for the shape have to account for the extraordinary effect of her cup; and their attempts to dilute its poison are admittedly feeble. Yet some interpreters, while remaining faithful to the essential goodness of the shape, thoughtfully condemn what she effects. Kenneth Allott explains this apparent contradiction by identifying the visionary draught with Rousseau's attempt "to realize the Ideal Vision in human love," an attempt which necessarily corrupts and weakens the sense of the Ideal. Rousseau's second Vision—the triumphal procession of Life whose captive train he joins—follows, then, as a consequence of his desire to quench his thirst for love incarnate; and this desire has eventually rooted him in a world he may never transcend, whether it be that of nature, as Bloom would have it, or of the imagination itself, as Woodman believes. ⟨. . .⟩

Bloom's typing of the shape as the "New Testament Great Whore" is one which, strangely enough, rests in part on Yeats's essay, "The Philosophy of Shelley's Poetry." Like most readers of *The Triumph of Life*, Bloom associates the shape with some aspect of the sun, but he does not regard this relationship as the guiltless one enjoyed by Apollo and the Witch of Atlas. Instead, drawing his argument in part from Yeats's essay, he characterizes the sun's power as "the being and the source of all tyrannies," and thus the shape, too, shares the solar cruelty. But Yeats himself, contrary to what Bloom says—that "Yeats had nothing to say of the Shape"—writes that the morning star is "personified as a woman" in *The Triumph of Life*, so that Yeats, who speaks so eloquently of the morning and evening star as the "symbol of love, or liberty, or wisdom, or beauty" in Shelley's poetry, could hardly have viewed the shape as "a diabolic parody of the Witch of Atlas," to whose wickedness poor Bradley succumbed. If Bradley was "taken in" by her, then so was Yeats. Yeats goes on to say that the morning star "leads Rousseau, the typical poet of *The Triumph of Life*, under the power of the destroying hunger of life, and it is the Morning Star that wars against the principle of evil in *Laon and Cythna.*" Here Yeats characteristically sees the sun as destructive, and incidentally causes some confusion in his ambiguous expression "leads . . . under the power." One might understand Yeats to mean that the morning star is the agent which *caused* Rousseau to submit to the power of life symbolized by the sun, or, conversely, that the morning star *kept guiding* Rousseau even whilst he was "under the power of the destroying hunger of life." ⟨. . .⟩

While I believe that Yeats was wrong to say that the sun's power is "the being and the source of all tyrannies" in Shelley's poetry, I contend that he was right to see the shape as a personification of "the most important, the most precise of all Shelley's symbols . . . the Morning and the Evening Star." I shall attempt both to revise Yeats's view of Shelley's solar imagery and to restore to the shape her proper glory.

Although Rousseau's vision takes place in "broad day" under the light of "the common Sun," he becomes aware of "a gentle trace / Of light diviner than the common Sun / Sheds on the common Earth." The presence of this diviner light is soon explained by his observation that "the bright omnipresence / Of morning" is flowing through the "orient cavern" of the mountain, and that the light of the sun is burning on the waters issuing from the cavern. In other words, Rousseau in his vision experiences the rising of one sun while the "common Sun" is at its zenith; and this is a clear indication that Shelley here distinguishes between two kinds of sun, the common and the visionary. It is therefore unfair to accept, with Bloom, Yeats's statement that "the sun's power is the being and the source of all tyrannies" in *The Triumph of Life* without recognizing a distinction between the reptile-spawning "common Sun" of *Adonais* and the "true Sun" of *The Triumph of Life.* ⟨. . .⟩

My argument is this: the shape must be in fact the morning star, Lucifer, still present at the rising of the sun. When the vision of the "fair shape" wanes, after Rousseau has touched his lips to the cup, her waning is compared to that of Lucifer, whose fading naturally occurs as the sun climbs higher. Rousseau can see the morning star clearly as long as the sun is low enough to stream through the "orient cavern" in the mountains, but even before sunrise "strike[s] the mountain tops," the "fairest planet" is blotted out by the "excess" of light from the ascendant sun, no longer the true or visionary sun.

—Linda E. Marshall, "The 'Shape All Light' in Shelley's *The Triumph of Life,*" *English Studies in Canada* 5, no. 1 (Spring 1979): pp. 49–52.

Daniel Hughes on the Destructive Connotations of the Word "Kindle"

[Daniel Hughes is the author of "Prometheus Made Capable Poet in Act One of *Prometheus Unbound*" (1978) and "Geoffrey Harman, Geoffrey Hartman" (1981). In the excerpt below from his article, "Kindling and Dwindling: The Poetic Process in Shelley," Hughes discusses the Rousseau passage in "The Triumph of Life" and the destructive connotations of the word "kindle."]

The valuable *Lexical Concordance* to Shelley's poetry, assembled by F. S. Ellis in 1892, lists seventy-one uses of *kindle* in Shelley's work, including seven appearances in his translations; only five uses of the word are to be taken literally, i.e. the actual lighting of a fire. ⟨. . .⟩ Clearly the job of work done by this word must be complex and varied, and the glosses that Ellis gives are quite inadequate to the work done in many cases—too many arbitrary and imprecise definitions are suggested. It is not the task of the lexicographer to do more than this, however, and the literary critic can only be grateful for a work like the Shelley *Concordance* and hope that he can turn the labor of the scholar to genuinely critical uses. Attempting, then, to see the meanings of Shelley's words in terms of the inter-relationships established in the poems themselves, we can see that the range of meaning *kindle* takes on in Shelley is very large and its functions complex. Generally speaking, the word can mean the awakening of the formal process of the poem and its hoped-for continuity, while it also establishes or leads to the Shelleyan hypostasis, most frequently symbolized by the female figure of Intellectual Beauty; it can also signify the act of creation in the universe itself, the beginning of intellection, sexual excitement, the inception of social and political revolution, and sometimes it refers to nature, particularly insofar as it is used of the dawn, a dawn that is often symbolic of the renewed processes of the poetry itself. Not all uses of the word are significant or worth examination, particularly in *Queen Mab* and *The Revolt of Islam* where the word is used to indicate a diffused excitement more than anything else. Nor do I wish to examine in this article all the interesting uses of the word in Shelley. I am primarily interested in it as pointing to Shelley's poetic strategies, with particular reference to his image of the fading coal as the condition of the poetic act, and all that act implies. ⟨. . .⟩

But in "The Triumph of Life," the whole pattern I have been tracing comes to a destructive and fascinating climax. It is true that, in the beginning of Rousseau's vision as he tells it, we discover the familiar inception of the full Shelleyan process:

> "In the April prime,
> When all the forest-tips began to burn
>
> "With *kindling* green, touched by the azure clime
> Of the young season, I was laid asleep
> Under a mountain, which from unknown time
>
> "Had yawned into a cavern, high and deep;"

We are familiar with this cluster and what it leads to, but an earlier appearance of our word in the poem might have warned us that all is not well. I have argued that *kindle* often points to awakened sexuality and that this sexuality is then translated into something intellective and poetic, in the manner of the Platonic ascent. But in the brilliant passage in "The Triumph" describing the destructive effects of sexual passion, there is no transcendence, no outward and upward movement:

> Maidens and youths fling their wild arms in air
> As their feet twinkle; they recede, and now

Bending within each other's atmosphere,

Kindle invisibly—and as they glow,
Like moths by light attracted and repelled,
Oft to their bright destruction come and go.

This "bright destruction" is the subject, I think, of the poem and the whole development of Rousseau's vision, lines 308-254, a tragic climax to Shelley's work, the ultimate dwindling of the Shelleyan process.

It is not my intention in this article to enter the lists in the continuing struggle among Shelley's critics as to the purpose of his great unfinished fragment, or to argue in detail about the meaning of Rousseau's vision. However, I do agree with Harold Bloom that the "Shape all light" who makes her appearance in line 352 must be understood as a malign, not a benign, figure, and that the drink she gives to Rousseau should be seen as completing the collapse from the essentiality of vision to the existentiality of human life. I think such a reading is supported by the scheme I have been tracing through Shelley. The Shape answers Rousseau's questions in this way:

" 'Arise and quench thy thirst', was her reply.
And as a shut lily stricken by the wand
Of dewy morning's vital alchemy,

"I rose; and, bending at her sweet command,
Touched with faint lips the cup she raised,
And suddenly my brain became as sand

"Where the first wave had more than half erased
The track of deer on desert Labrador;"

But the Shelleyan process is aborted here, defeated, the kindling comes to a premature and ironic end; the "cold bright car" of the Chariot of Life returns. We need not worry whether the disaster was fully apparent to Shelley. Certainly, the Shape appears to have all the kindling characteristics of the figure of Intellectual Beauty, but the apparently casual cliché, "*quench* thy thirst," reveals the extent of the collapse. *Quench* is Shelley's antonym to *kindle*, and stands in the same relation to the destruction of the creative process, the extinguishing of the fading coal, that *kindle* does to its awakening. The one thing that should not happen to Rousseau-Shelley's thirst is its quenching, but quenched it is, and the rest of "The Triumph of Life" and the last few weeks of Shelley's life bear testimony to this outcome, both within the poem and within the cancelling waters off Viareggio. ⟨...⟩

It is this quality of perpetual renewal that Shelley yearns for and which the "quenching" of "The Triumph of Life" so conspicuously lacks. The aroused coal of his inspiration, whether this took an intellective or a sexual, a political or a mystical turn, sought ways to sustain itself between the poles of a sudden kindling and an inevitable quenching or collapse. In his curse on the Lord Chancellor, these key words come together in a single line. Shelley curses Lord Eldon by the very qualities the Chancellor has sought to deny:

> By those infantine smiles of happy light,
>   Which were a fire within a stranger's hearth,
> *Quenched* even when *kindled*, in untimely night
>   Hiding the promise of a lovely birth.

> —Daniel Hughes, "Kindling and Dwindling: The Poetic Process in Shelley," *Keats-Shelley Journal* 13 (Winter 1964): pp. 15–16, 23–24, 25.

FRED L. MILNE ON THE RELEVANCE OF SHELLEY'S "DEFENCE OF POETRY"

[Fred L. Milne is the author of "Numerology, Water-Imagery, and Transmutation: Some Aspects of Shelley's 'Adonais'" (1988) and "Love-Strife and Night Motifs in Christopher Marlowe's 'Hero & Leander'" (1996). In the excerpt below from his article, "The Eclipsed Imagination in Shelley's 'The Triumph of Life,'" Milne discusses the poem in the context of Shelley's *A Defence of Poetry*, a critical work that emphasizes the force of the imagination as a guiding principle against the enslaving "dominance of reason" in the everyday world of appearances.]

Shelley's "The Triumph of Life" explores the consequences befalling the mind's perception of reality when the light of imagination is eclipsed or displaced by another intellectual light as the principal mode of knowledge. But the apparent failure of imagination is not depicted as necessary or final in "The Triumph." Contrary to some recent readings, the poem does not reveal "the latent negativity of the imagination." Nor does the poem reflect Shelley's "loss of faith in the world of imagination"; it is not the "recantation" of a "poet who has rejected poetry," nor is it a "suicidal" poem. Rather, "The Triumph" reiterates one of the central ideas in *A Defence of Poetry*: the imperative need for imagination as a guiding force against the excessive dominance of reason, termed in the *Defence* "the owl-winged faculty of calculation." Without imagination man is enslaved to a phenomenal or empirical view of reality, a problem Shelley thought particularly acute when he wrote the *Defence*: "The cultivation of those sciences which have enlarged the limits of the empire of man over the external world has for want of the poetical faculty proportionally circumscribed those of the internal world; and man, having enslaved the elements, remains himself a slave." "The Triumph" depicts the intellectual enslavement resulting when the primacy of imagination is displaced in the mind by the interposition of an intellectual power that eclipses and usurps imagination's light. The consequence, as two recent critics have argued, is a type of purgatorial living death. Yet such a state is neither inevitable nor inescapable. "The Triumph" implicitly points toward the means of reviving imaginative vision, for its apparent failure reflects, according to Shelley, man's prior embrace of selfhood, an act negating imagination's power. Consequently, the only light left to guide the mind is reason, without imagination a cold and loveless power, its knowledge limited to the empirical. Restoration of imagination demands redirection of man's will, rejection of selfhood in favor of love, defined in the *Defence* as "a going out of our own nature and an identification of ourselves with the beautiful which exists in thought, action, or person, not our own." That essential point is made explicit in "The Triumph" through Rousseau's narrative, for it serves as an object lesson to the poem's speaker of one who in life did not make the necessary commitment of will.

The sunrise opening "The Triumph" is generally recognized as auspicious in Shelley's poetry, and it introduces the imagination theme:

> Swift as a Spirit hastening to his task
>> Of glory & of good, the Sun sprang forth

> Rejoicing in his splendour, & the mask
>   Of darkness fell from the awakened Earth.

As in *Prometheus Unbound*, the movement here is from night to day, from darkness to illumination, representing a crucial awakening. The effect of the sunrise is identical to that in *Prometheus* where Asia states "Prometheus shall arise / Henceforth the sun of this rejoicing world." The rise of the Promethean sun parts "the veil, by those who were, called life"—an act of which the Spirit of the Hour says: "The loathsome mask has fallen," revealing a world pervaded by love made visible by the Promethean sun. The sunrise that opens "The Triumph" likewise removes "the mask of darkness" as all elements in nature "Rise as the Sun their father rose" in response to that joyous event.

The positive effect of the sun's initial appearance in "The Triumph" is incompatible with Harold Bloom's suggestion that it represents a Wordsworthian fading of visionary power into "the light of common day." In function, the sun symbolizes imagination which "strips the veil of familiarity from the world and lays bare the naked and sleeping beauty." That identification gains plausibility in light of Shelley's use of the sun as symbol of imagination, particularly in his later writing. In *Prometheus Unbound* the sun assumes that symbolic connotation through its association with Prometheus, generally interpreted as personifying the imaginative power in man. Explicit use of the sun as symbol of imagination occurs in a verse fragment appearing just prior to the draft of a lyric passage intended for *Prometheus* in the Bixby-Huntington notebook:

> Hold—divine image
> Eclipsed Sun—Planet without a beam
> Wilt thou offend the Sun thou emblemest
> By blotting out the light of written thought?

Eclipse of the sun by the moon symbolizes eclipse of the imagination, the "divine image" in man expressed through "written thought" or poetry. Because the moon, the "Planet without a beam," should rightly receive its light from the sun, serving thereby as a reflected emblem of the "divine image," its interposition before the sun is offensive because it blots out the "divine image." Instead of reflecting the sun, the moon negates its light. Such an eclipse violates the moon's function as emblemizer of the sun as the lesser, inherently cold light imposes itself before the greater, warming light.

—Fred L. Milne, "The Eclipsed Imagination in Shelley's 'The Triumph of Life,'" *Studies in English Literature 1500–1900* 21, no. 4 (Autumn 1981): pp. 681–84.

JOHN MORILLO ON THE POEM AS SHELLEY'S RESPONSE TO SOUTHEY

[John Morillo is the author of "Seditious Anger: Achilles, James Stuart, and Jacobite Politics in Pope's *Iliad* Translation" (1995). In the excerpt below from his article, "Vegetating Radicals and Imperial Politics: Shelley's *Triumph of Life* as Revision of Southey's *Pilgrimage to Waterloo*," Morillo discusses the poem as Shelley's response to Southey's narrative of the failure of the French Revolution.]

From at least as early as 1817, Percy Shelley's contentious print relationship with Robert Southey combined literary appropriation and allusion with political critique. In late poems like "The Witch of Atlas," Marilyn Butler has argued, Shelley's "favourite devices, his allegorical journeys and mythological landscapes, plainly derive from Southey." Both Butler and Kenneth Neill Cameron have focussed on the political motivation behind Shelley's interest in Southey's writings, pitting Shelley's radicalism against the increasingly conservative and public Toryism of Southey in his overtly politicized role as England's poet laureate. Cameron has described how, in June 1817, Shelley was provoked by Southey's *Quarterly Review* attacks on him to seek specific redress, how "until 1821 Shelley was . . . seeking an occasion to answer Southey's veiled and rather underhanded attack."

Whereas Cameron sees *Adonais* as Shelley's ultimate reply to Southey, I will argue that the most comprehensive critique of Southey's abuse of laureate powers comes in Shelley's final, fragmentary work, *The Triumph of Life* (1822). By reading Shelley's poem as a direct counter-response to Southey's *The Poet's Pilgrimage to Waterloo* (1816), I mean to show how the laureate poem furnished

Shelley not only with specific literary devices to appropriate and manipulate, but also with compelling political reasons to answer Southey's officially sanctioned narrative of the failure of the French Revolution. Shelley's *Triumph* reveals how Southey's *Pilgrimage*, despite its anti-war sentiment, participates in a Tory ideology that naturalizes imperialism as the necessary result of England's cultural history, an ideology as ultimately destructive as the Napoleonic conquest Southey overtly condemns. ⟨...⟩

In both *The Excursion* and Southey's *Pilgrimage* Shelley saw similar post-revolutionary misconstructions of recent English and European history. *The Poets' Pilgrimage*, like *The Triumph*, ties an evaluation of Rousseauist thought to the fall of Napoleon. Shelley directly challenges Southey's vision of Rousseau as the malignant spirit of the French Revolution and of Napoleon as the satanic instigator of its downfall.

Southey's verse narrative describes his 1815 journey to the Belgian battlefield and his ensuing vision of a post-Napoleonic world's fortunate fall under English imperial hegemony and moral stewardship. In *The Pilgrimage*, we find not only all of the narrative details relevant to the kind of poem Shelley writes, but also the specific language of many of Shelley's stanzas. Southey's first-person narrator, like Shelley's, falls into a dream-vision in which the action is concentrated into scenes that correspond remarkably to the progress of Shelley's poem. For example, Southey's vision includes: 1) a plain where "innumerable crowds / Like me were on their destined journey bent . . . a motley multitude of old and young"; 2) a meeting with a guide figure which culminates in the request to "Instruct me then . . . for thou should'st know / From whence I came and whither I must go"; 3) a voyage to a stream in the woods where a second luminous vision-within-a-vision is "Raised on the stream a shower of sparkling light"; and 4) a "Well of Life" from which the guide-figure asks the narrator to drink and purify his vision. When Southey's Christian narrator drinks from this Well of Life flowing from "the Rock of Ages," he rises with renovated soul to a blessedly uncomplicated vision of England, now free of Napoleon, extending its empire eastward to India and beyond. Southey's autobiographical *Pilgrimage* centers on a dream allegory provoked by the fate of Napoleon and France, and culminates in a glowing vision of England's divinely-guided, worldwide imperial expansion. Most important, however, is the fact that Southey's vision matches the post-revolutionary, post-Napoleonic European context of *The Triumph of Life*, another story told by Rousseau about Napoleon, poets, and power.

This reading proposes more than a critical addition to the many earlier source studies of *The Triumph of Life*. Although I maintain that Southey's poem is essential to *The Triumph*'s enigmatic texture, I locate its importance to Shelley in political and historical terms. Southey's poem engages ideological and historical concerns about revolution, history, and empire, issues raised in studies of *The Triumph of Life* by critics such as David Quint and Orrin N. C. Wang. While recognizing the significant influence of Paul de Man to much modern work on *The Triumph*, especially when it comes to Rousseau's role, I question his over-generalized epistemological conclusion about the impossibility of historical knowledge, as well as Hillis Miller's similar sense of the poem as a "self-deconstruction" and epitome of indeterminacy. As a reply to Southey, *The Triumph of Life* suggests instead a Shelley who remains confident that he can account for both how and why certain highly motivated claims to historical knowledge can be evaluated for their accuracy—and for their consequences.

—John Morillo, "Vegetating Radicals and Imperial Politics: Shelley's *Triumph of Life* as Revision of Southey's *Pilgrimage to Waterloo*," *Keats-Shelley Journal* 43 (1994): pp. 117–20.

Works by
Percy Bysshe Shelley

The Necessity of Atheism. 1811.

An Address to the Irish People. 1812.

Proposals for an Association. 1812.

Declaration of Rights. 1812.

A Letter to Lord Ellenborough. 1812.

A Vindication of Natural Diet. 1813.

Queen Mab: A Philosophical Poem: with Notes. 1813.

A Refutation of Deism. 1813.

Alastor; or, The Spirit of Solitude: and Other Poems. 1816.

History of a Six Weeks' Tour through a Part of France, Switzerland, Germany. 1817.

A Proposal for Putting Reform to the Vote. 1817.

An Address to the People on the Death of Princess Charlotte. 1817.

Laon and Cythna; or, The Revolution of the Golden City. 1817.

The Revolt of Islam. 1818.

The Banquet (a translation of Plato's *Symposium*). 1818

Julian and Maddalo. 1818.

"The Masque of Anarchy." 1819.

"Peter Bell the Third." 1819.

Rosalind and Helen, A Modern Eclogue; with Other Poems. 1819.

A Philosophical View of Reform. c. 1819.

The Cenci: A Tragedy in Five Acts. 1819.

Prometheus Unbound. 1820.

Oedipus Tyrannus, or Swell-foot the Tyrant. 1820.

The Witch of Atlas. 1820.

Epipsychidion. 1821.

A Defence of Poetry. 1820.

Adonais. 1821.

Hellas. 1821.

The Triumph of Life. 1822.

The Complete Works of Percy Bysshe Shelley, edited by Roger Ingpen and Walter E. Peck. 10 vols. 1926–1930.

Shelley's "Prometheus Unbound": A Variorum Edition, edited by Lawrence John Zillman. 1959.

The Letters of Percy Bysshe Shelley, edited by Frederick L. Jones. 2 vols. 1964.

The Complete Poetical Works of Percy Bysshe Shelley, edited by Neville Rogers. 1971.

Works about
Percy Bysshe Shelley

Abbey, Lloyd. *Destroyer and Preserver: Shelley's Poetic Skepticism.* Lincoln: University of Nebraska Press, 1979.

Abrams, Meyer H. *The Correspondent Breeze.* New York: Norton, 1984.

Allot, Miriam, ed. *Essays on Shelley.* Totowa, N.J.: Barnes and Noble, 1982.

Baker, Carols. *Shelley's Major Poetry.* Princeton, N.J.: Princeton University Press, 1948.

Bandy, Melanie. *Mind Forg'd Manacles: Evil in the Poetry of Blake and Shelley.* Tuscaloosa: University of Alabama Press, 1981.

Blank, G. Kim. *The New Shelley: Later Twentieth Century Views.* New York: St. Martin's Press, 1991.

Bloom, Harold. *Shelley's Mythmaking.* New Haven: Yale University Press, 1959.

———, ed. *Romanticism and Consciousness: Essays in Criticism.* New York: W. W. Norton, 1970.

Bostetter, Edward. *The Romantic Ventriloquists: Wordsworth, Coleridge, Shelley, Keats, Byron.* Seattle: University of Washington Press, 1963.

Butter, Peter. *Shelley's Idols of the Cave.* New York: Haskell House, 1969.

Curran, Stuart. *Shelley's Annus Mirabilis: The Maturing of an Epic Vision.* San Marion, Calif.: Huntingdon Library, 1975.

———. *Poetic Form and British Romanticism.* Oxford: Oxford University Press, 1986.

Duerksen, Ronald. *Shelley's Poetry of Involvement.* New York: St. Martin's Press, 1988.

Duff, David. *Romance and Revolution: Shelley and the Politics of a Genre.* Cambridge: Cambridge University Press, 1994.

Duffy, Edward. *Rousseau in England: The Context for Shelley's Critique of the Enlightenment.* Berkeley and Los Angeles: University of California Press, 1979.

Gallant, Christine. *Shelley's Ambivalence.* New York: St. Martin's Press, 1989.

Grabo, Carl. *A Newton Among Poets: Shelley's Use of Science in Prometheus Unbound.* Chapel Hill: University of North Carolina Press, 1930.

Guinn, J. P. *Shelley's Political Thought.* The Hague: Mouton, 1969.

Hall, Jean. *The Transforming Image: A Study of Shelley's Major Poetry.* Urbana: University of Illinois Press, 1980.

Hoagwood, Terence. *Skepticism and Ideology: Shelley's Political Prose and Its Philosophical Context from Bacon to Marx.* Iowa City: University of Iowa Press, 1988.

Hodgart, Patrica. *A Preface to Shelley.* London: Longman, 1988.

Hogle, Jerrold E. *Shelley's Process: Radical Transference and the Development of His Major Works.* New York: Oxford University Press, 1988.

Holmes, Richard. *Shelley: The Pursuit.* New York: Elisabeth Sifton Boosk, 1974.

Jones, Steven E. *Shelley's Satire: Violence, Exhortation, and Authority.* DeKalb: Northern Illinois University Press, 1994.

Keach, William. *Shelley's Style.* London: Methuen, 1984.

King-Hele, Desmond. *Shelley: His Thought and Work.* 3d ed. Cranbury, N.J.: Associated University Presses, 1984.

Kurtz, B.J. *The Pursuit of Death: A Study of Shelley's Poetry.* New York: Octagon, 1970.

Leighton, Angela. *Shelley and the Sublime: An Interpretation of the Major Poems.* Cambridge: Cambridge University Press, 1984.

McNiece, Gerald. *Shelley and the Revolutionary Idea.* Cambridge, Mass.: Harvard University Press, 1969.

Morton, Timothy. *Shelley and the Revolution in Taste: The Body and the Natural World.* Cambridge: Cambridge University Press, 1994.

Notopoulos, James. *The Platonism of Shelley: A Study of Platonism and the Poetic Mind.* New York: Octagon, 1969.

Perkins, David. *The Quest for Permanence: The Symbolism of Wordsworth, Shelley, and Keats.* Cambridge, Mass.: Harvard University Press, 1965.

Pulos, C. E. *The Deep Truth: A Study of Shelley's Skepticism.* Lincoln: University of Nebraska Press, 1954.

Reiman, Donald. *Shelley's "The Triumph of Life": A Critical Study.* Urbana: University of Illinois Press, 1965.

Robinson, C. E. *Shelley and Byron: The Snake and the Eagle Wreathed in Fight.* Baltimore: Johns Hopkins University Press, 1976.

Schulze, E. J. *Shelley's Theory of Poetry: A Reappraisal.* The Hague: Mouton, 1966.

Scrivener, Michael. *Radical Shelley: The Philosophical Anarchism and Utopian Thought of Percy Bysshe Shelley.* Princeton: Princeton University Press, 1982.

Sperry, Stuart. *Shelley's Major Verse: The Narrative and Dramatic Poetry.* Cambridge, Mass.: Harvard University Press, 1988.

Stovall, Floyd. *Desire and Restraint in Shelley.* Durham, N.C.: Duke University Press, 1931.

Tetreault, Ronald. *The Poetry of Life: Shelley and Literary Form.* Toronto: University of Toronto Press, 1987.

Ulmer, William. *Shelleyan Eros: The Rhetoric of Romantic Love.* Princeton: Princeton University Press, 1990.

Wasserman, E. R. *Shelley: A Critical Reading.* Baltimore: Johns Hopkins University Press, 1971.

Webb, Timothy. *Shelley: A Voice Not Understood.* Manchester: Manchester University Press, 1977.

Wilson, Milton. *Shelley's Later Poetry: A Study of His Prophetic Imagination.* New York: Columbia University Press, 1959.

Woodman, Ross Grieg. *The Apocalyptic Vision in the Poetry of Shelley.* Toronto: University of Toronto Press, 1964.

Woodring, Carl. *Politics in English Romantic Poetry.* Cambridge, Mass.: Harvard University Pres, 1970.

Wright, J. *Shelley's Myth of Metaphor.* Athens: University of Georgia Press, 1970.

Young, A. *Shelley and Nonviolence.* The Hague: Mouton, 1975.

Index of
Themes and Ideas

sonnet, 54, 55, 56, 57–58, 61; spiritual redemption in, 59–61; structure of, 64–65; thematic analysis of, 49–53; transformation of poetic anxiety in, 63–65; wind as breath and spirit in, 49, 50–51, 59, 61–63, 65; wind as God-figure in, 60–61; wind as intimation in, 49; wind as renewal in, 49, 53, 65–67; wind's divine power in, 53; and Wordsworth, 9–10, 57, 58 views on, 88, 96–112; and Dante, 11, 93, 95, 98; death in, 93–94; and *A Defence of Poetry,* 107–10; as dream-vision, 91, 93; Lord Eldon in, 107; exhaustion and fruitless effort in, 93; fatalism in, 95; female soul-figure in, 99; and Gnosticism, 10; and ideology, 99–101; imagination in, 107–10; "kindle" in, 104–7; light and sun in, 96, 97–98, 101–4, 106, 108–9; love in, 101; Lucifer in, 104; medieval elements in, 91–92, 93; moon in, 109; morning star in, 103, 104; pageant in, 92, 93–94, 99, 100; as response to Southey, 110–12; and Rousseau, 94–95, 98–101, 102, 103, 104, 105, 106–7, 111, 112; sexuality in, 105; shadow in, 99–100, 101; sunrise opening of, 108–9; thematic analysis of, 91–95; "triumph" in, 92; truth in, 96–98; and Wordsworth, 8; Yeats in, 102–3

"VICTOR AND CAZIRE," 13

"WITCH OF ATLAS, THE," 39, 110

ZASTROZZ, 13